Is God Helpless?

Suffering and the Sovereignty of God

Peter Cotterell was born an identical twin in Malta. His family returned to England very shortly after his birth, following the death of his father. He worked successively as an office boy, a research scientist at Kodak, a school teacher and part-time lecturer in physics at Brunel University. He holds degrees in physics, theology and linguistics and is a Fellow of the Institute of Linguistics and of the Royal Society of Arts.

A significant part of Dr Cotterell's life was the 19 years he spent in Ethiopia, sharing in the rich faith of Ethiopian Christians, and witnessing their fortitude during almost unbroken persecution and during periods of drought.

From 1976 until his retirement in 1995 he lectured at the London Bible College, for the last six years as Principal.

He is married to Geraldine, a Geordie, and they have two daughters, one an RE teacher in Birmingham, and the other an architect. This is his fifteenth book.

IS GOD HELPLESS?

Suffering and the Sovereignty of God

Peter Cotterell

TRIANGLE

First published in Great Britain 1996
Triangle
SPCK
Holy Trinity Church
Marylebone Road
London NW1 4DU

British Library Cataloguing-in-Publication Data
A catalogue record for this book is available from the British Library
ISBN 0-281-04896-7

Typeset by Dorwyn Ltd., Portsmouth, Hants
Printed in Great Britain by Biddles Ltd.,Guildford and King's Lynn

Contents

IS GOD HELPLESS?
Suffering and the Sovereignty of God

Introduction

Screwtape, warning the junior tempter Wormwood, on the danger of faith:

> Do not be deceived, Wormwood. Our cause is never more in danger than when a human, no longer desiring, but still intending to do our Enemy's will, looks round upon a universe from which every trace of Him seems to have vanished, and asks why he has been forsaken, and still obeys.
>
> C.S. Lewis, *The Screwtape Letters*

There are two complaints that we all make at some time: 'It isn't fair!' and 'Why does God allow it?' These two complaints form the framework for this book. They signal most people's opinion of life: that although life often does seem to be fair, there are plenty of times when it does not. And since we expect life to be fair, we expect God to step in, somehow, to make it fair. Most often he doesn't seem to do it.

Anyone with eyes to see and ears to hear will know that life is terribly unfair, and that it is the ordinary person, the unimportant person, the poor person, the powerless person, in other words the vast majority of the world's population, who has to bear it all.

And yet, oddly enough, most people believe in God. Not everyone believes in a particular God – the God of Christianity or of any one of the other religions – but still God. There is this belief deep down inside most of us that there must be someone out there, the one who made all this, someone who is responsible for it all, someone who has the kind of power that we haven't got, and who could and should keep things fair.

Christianity doesn't teach that God is going to do that for us, and it doesn't teach that life is fair. Even in the Old Testament, in the psalms, for example, and especially in the book of Proverbs, the writers recognise that although good people *ought* to be rewarded, often they are not, because wealthier, more influential, less honest people lie to them and cheat and exploit them.

But Christianity does *not* simply shrug its shoulders and walk off with a muttered apology: 'Tough. Wish life could be better, but that's the way it is.' It does have an explanation of why things aren't fair, of why God doesn't intervene (or at least only sometimes intervenes), and how life could be more fair.

There's a whole chapter in this book on pain, illness and death, and another chapter on prayer: why so many prayers (for someone to be healed, for example) don't get the answers we want. But I'll admit right here that this is not an easy book to read. Even so, the subject is important and the struggle to follow me through should be worthwhile.

Of course I'm not the first theologian to tackle the question of human suffering. Human suffering is a problem only to those who believe in God, and for them the issue is more than a question of human happiness or human misery: it is a question of the righteousness of God. If life is unfair how does that square with the existence of a righteous God? The whole issue of human suffering then receives the label *theodicy*, 'the righteousness of God', and in some sense becomes the search to preserve the notion of a righteous God in this miserable world.

The general question of the existence of evil becomes problematic when it is associated with the idea of a righteous God. The eighteenth-century philosopher David Hume expressed the problem neatly:

Is God willing to prevent evil, but unable to do so?
    In this case God is impotent.
Is God able to prevent evil, but unwilling to do so?
    In this case God is malevolent.
Is God able to prevent evil and willing to prevent evil?
    In this case why is there suffering at all?[1]

Although the problem of evil is a universal problem, the problem of theodicy is not: it obviously depends on a belief in a God who is omnipotent and beneficent and moral. It also assumes that this morality means the same as our morality: that what God considers to be evil is what we consider to be evil, and, more importantly, that what we consider to be evil, God also considers to be evil. A little thought will make the point clear. We may naively consider that toothache is an evil, but without it we would not be aware of tooth decay. The pain has a purpose and this might lead to the conclusion that, after all, pain is a good.

In fact this indicates one argument that some philosophers have used to deal more generally with the problem of human suffering. If it could be shown that my suffering here results in good elsewhere then maybe that suffering is brought by God whose intention is beneficent.

The argument is theoretically plausible, but it is very difficult for us to see that the suffering produced in the destruction of the capital city of the republic of Chechnya, which took place while this book was being written, or even worse, the massacre of the Jews in the holocaust, has produced any good remotely commensurate with the people's suffering. Of course there were great acts of heroism, of self-denial, of self-sacrifice, in both those occurrences. But the sheer scale of the horror militates against the proposed solution. The tears are too many, the hurts too deep, the losses too great.

The philosopher Richard Swinburn has in fact attempted to justify God, to preserve his righteousness, by analytically, clinically, and impersonally examining the cries of pain that have been torn from human beings by their torturers. But here Christian compassion parts company with cold philosophy. It must surely be a sign of a corrupt mind that it can coldly weigh in the balances of philosophical judgment the screams of pain and the purposes of God. For me it is impossible, it is impossible to think of God as willing those cries of pain for any reason whatever. The cry of pain is both a measure of the suffering of the individual and the condemnation of the one causing it. If it should be argued that it is God causing it, then one must say that throughout history a great cry against the righteousness of God has gone up continually, and my voice is joined with those of the millions.

But I do not believe that these real sufferings of ours are willed by God or caused by God. It is my task to explore this subject, but from my own perspective of hurt and pain and compassion. I have known much pain myself. I have seen more pain in the lives of others. I lived and walked through the pains of the Ethiopian people in famine and in war. And it is out of the tears that I have shed in all of this that my search for some answer to human suffering must come.

1
Why Bad Things Happen to Good People

Screwtape to Wormwood on war, human suffering, death:

> They, of course, do tend to regard death as the prime evil and survival as the greatest good. But that is because we have taught them to do so. Do not let us be infected by our own propaganda. I know it seems strange that your chief aim at the moment should be the very same thing for which the patient's lover and his mother are praying – namely his bodily safety. But so it is; you should be guarding him like the apple of your eye. If he dies now you lose him.
>
> C.S. Lewis, The Screwtape Letters

The title of this chapter is taken from the book written back in 1981 by a Jewish Rabbi, Harold Kushner. His son, Aaron, was afflicted with a disease called progeria, premature and rapidly progressive ageing. The doctor told him that Aaron would never grow much beyond three feet in height, would have no hair on his head or on his body, and would almost certainly die in his early teens. Rabbi Kushner wrote of his feelings:

> What I mostly felt that day was a deep aching sense of unfairness. It didn't make sense. I had been a good person. I had tried to do what was right in the sight of God. More than that, I was living a more religiously committed life than most people I knew, people who had large, healthy families. . . . How could this be happening to my family? If God existed, if He was minimally fair, let alone loving and forgiving, how could He do this to me?

And maybe you feel the same about some experience of your own.

We can divide human tragedies into two types: individual tragedy, like Rabbi Kushner's, and mass tragedy, like the famine in Ethiopia in the 1970s and 1980s, when something like a million people starved to death, or the World War II holocaust when around six million Jews were systematically put to death.

INDIVIDUAL TRAGEDIES

A good many years ago, in a quiet suburb of London, I was taking one of my children to school. We had almost got there. The school was on my left. Glancing out of the car window to the right I saw two people, struggling together. I quickly stopped the car, hurried Anne into the safety of the school playground, ran back across the road. By now the two figures were sprawled across the grass verge, blood everywhere, both alive, but barely breathing. Someone dashed to the nearest house to phone for an ambulance and the police. We did what we could for the man and the woman, but their injuries, obviously inflicted by the long knife lying on the pavement now, were horrific. The ambulance came, the police came, and eventually we discovered what had happened.

These two had been living together for some years, although they weren't married. They had a little girl. Each day the woman took the little girl to school, but on this morning she had told the man that she was finished with him: she was going to take their child and leave him. He waited until she left home as usual, to take their girl to school. He went to the kitchen drawer, found a sharp knife, followed her up the road, waited until she came out of the school and then plunged the knife into her back. And then he cut his own throat.

She was dead on arrival at the hospital. He recovered, to stand trial for murder: the sentence was life imprisonment. One life was ended, another life was ruined, but at least in some sense it was their quarrel. But inside the school was their daughter, and someone had to tell her that the little bit of security that she had known that morning was gone. All of it. And I don't know what happened to her in the years after that terrible morning.

For some nineteen years my wife and I were missionaries in Ethiopia. Perhaps the hardest experience of my life was something that happened there. I had to conduct the funeral service at our mission chapel in Addis Ababa for a young Australian doctor. He had come out to us on a short-term appointment. He was sent with a medical team into the hot lowlands over towards Somalia. One morning he was setting up his tent ready for the operations he would expect to carry out that day. A Somali Muslim came up behind him and killed him with a single fierce thrust of a dagger.

The two nurses with him loaded his body into their Land Rover and drove him back to Addis Ababa. Perhaps an hour before the funeral service was due to begin I went into the chapel to see that everything was in order. Seated on a bench was one of those nurses, doubled over, her head cradled in her hands, the tears streaming between her fingers, as she said over and over again: 'It doesn't make sense, it just doesn't make sense.'

Or take the death of Dr Margaret FitzHerbert. A redoubtable lady, she had been awarded a medal by Haile Selassie and the OBE by the British Government. She had devoted herself to the Ethiopian people. She drove an ancient Volkswagen, which always carried with it a quite appalling smell; she was rarely without some poor unfortunate man or woman whom she was taking to hospital, probably someone with leprosy and so almost certainly with three or four other illnesses, and again almost certainly with horrific suppurating wounds. Margaret dedicated herself to helping people who suffered from leprosy. In fact a year or more before she died she told me that she had herself contracted leprosy. But she didn't die of leprosy. She had a brain haemorrhage.

They brought her to Addis Ababa and I sat with her in the hospital. She was almost totally paralysed, she couldn't speak and yet her brain was as active as ever. And I shall never, never forget sitting by her bedside as she slept, watching her wake up and her tears begin as she realised her condition. Helpless. Unable to communicate. It didn't make sense. It wasn't fair.

Or take Julie and Mike who were students at London Bible College. She was stunningly beautiful. Mike was all man, but gentle with it, and full of faith. They got engaged, but even before they could be married he was diagnosed as having a rare form of cancer. We didn't really think that he could be strong enough for the date they had planned their wedding, but Mike made it! And then followed the desperate struggle with his illness. He was in and out of hospital, and the doctors and nurses were perennially amazed that Mike was still alive. Yes, he was all man. Between them, the nurses and the doctors and the treatments and the prayers, they gradually seemed to get on top of the disease. The tumours were shrinking. Mike came back to college to report on progress; yes, still far from well, but getting stronger by the day.

And then the cancer struck again: in the brain, this time. And now the road was all downhill. Mike died. We were all shattered that the battle we had thought to be won was now lost. I talked to Julie, later. She told me, with total honesty, that she had cried out to God: 'Why? Why should this happen to Mike?' But Mike had never asked that. She told me that when in her exhaustion, she had cried out 'Why him?', Mike had replied simply 'Why not me?'

MASS TRAGEDIES

And then there are the great mass tragedies. Here it is difficult even to start. When I began writing, the terrible massacres in Rwanda were still going on. The civil war in the former Yugoslavia had devastated much of the country and ruined the lives, destroyed the hopes of hundreds of thousands of very ordinary people. In the former Soviet Union, the battle for the Chechin capital, Grozny, had left the city itself in ruins, with hundreds of thousands homeless, and tens of thousands killed – ordinary Chechin people. They are the ones who seem always to pay the price, like the holocaust victims, the six million killed for the sake of Aryan 'purity'.

In 1995 we observed the fiftieth anniversary of the Russian liberation of the Nazi extermination camp at Auschwitz, where one and a half million people, the vast majority Jewish, were gassed and then cremated. Their story was told fifty years on through the television screen. The Nazis used Jewish labour teams to service the camps, to move the bodies from the gas chamber to the cremation furnaces. Among the crowd of newly arrived, exhausted, frightened Jews one of the work team saw a woman he knew. He knew also the lies these people were being told: 'Take off your filthy clothes, you will have a bath, and a refreshing drink, and then a holiday.' He told her the truth: in an hour they would all be dead. She could scarcely believe it: and then began to move around her companions, warning them of their fate. And they wouldn't, couldn't, believe it: no one could do that to helpless women, men, children. The Nazi guards saw what was happening. They seized the woman, paraded the work team, and then in front of their horrified eyes tortured her horribly until she pointed out the man who had told her. He was seized and thrown alive into the furnace. And then she was killed.

Still for me the ultimate example is the tragedy of the Welsh mining village of Aberfan. Up behind the village was the slag heap, the mountain of earth excavated from the nearby coal mine. Everyone knew that the slag heap was unsafe. The danger had been reported to the authorities. It was raining on the morning of 21 October 1966, and two inspectors from the local authority stood in the rain looking at the slag heap. As they watched, the mountain of mud and stone began to move, faster and faster, sliding down the mountainside, not merely onto the village, but directly onto the little school. One hundred and thirty-eight children died at their desks, buried alive under a torrent of mud.

These true stories set the agenda for this book. The problem of pain is an old one, and the question 'Why?' is a universal one. All too often Christian responses and the answers of the philosophers have been buried in great tomes and hidden away in language that only scholars can understand. But it is we, the ordinary people of the world, who feel the pain most, and ask the question most poignantly. In looking for a Christian answer I've tried not to dodge the difficult questions, or to take refuge in learned footnotes.

2
What Religions Say

Screwtape advising Wormwood on the characteristics of contemporary human thinking:

> Your man has been accustomed, ever since he was a boy, to have a dozen incompatible philosophies dancing about together inside his head. He doesn't think of doctrines as primarily 'true' or 'false', but as 'academic' or 'practical', 'outworn' or 'contemporary', 'conventional' or 'ruthless'.
> C.S. Lewis, *The Screwtape Letters*

BUT THEY ALL SAY IT DIFFERENTLY

It is often said that all religions are really the same. That's usually said by people who know very little about religions. In fact religions agree about very little. They don't all believe in God: Gautama the Buddha ('the enlightened one') produced an explanation of the world and a way for people to follow, but neither of them contained any mention of God. Confucius, too, left God out: he was more concerned with tradition and with the ancestors. If Marxism is a religion (and I think it is), then it is even possible to have an atheistic religion.

Religions don't all agree that God created the world, or even that the world was created. Religions don't all agree that we should love one another. Some religions teach that we should love our own kind, but have no need to love people from another race. Hinduism had the practice of *thuggee* (hence our word 'thug'), which meant the ritual murder of people who strayed into their territory. The harsh religion of the Danakil people of East Africa still allows for the murder and mutilation of the unwary traveller.

However, religions do all agree that life should make sense but it doesn't. Nihilism, therefore, which recognises that life doesn't appear to make sense, but which goes on to say 'Too bad, but that's the way it is', is not a religion. It is the denial of religion. In fact, it seems to me that we can define a religion in terms of a belief that although life does not appear to make sense it can still be made to make sense. Apparent meaninglessness can be explained. As the Vatican Council put it:

> Men look to their religions for an answer to the unsolved riddles of human existence. The problems that weigh heavily on the hearts of men are the same today as in the ages past. What is man? What is the meaning and purpose of life? What is upright behaviour, and what is sinful? Where does suffering originate, and what end does it serve . . .? And finally, what is the ultimate mystery, beyond human explanation, which embraces our entire existence, from which we take our origin and towards which we tend?[1]

It is a fact that all religions try to provide meaningful, understandable, logical answers to the fundamental questions about life, the questions that at some time or other, in some form or other, we all ask: 'Who am I?' 'Where did I come from?' 'Where am I going to?' 'Why?' You can ask the same set of questions about other people and about the world: 'Who are you?' 'What is it?' 'Where did it come from?' 'Where is it going to?' 'Why?' These are, in fact, the very questions that the Vatican Council identified.

THE EXPLANATION GIVEN BY HINDUISM

If we concentrate our attention on the answers given by religions to these questions it is easy to see that they are *not* all saying the same thing. Hinduism gives what is probably the most complete explanation of human suffering: it is due to *karma* accumulated from previous existences. According

12

to Hinduism there is an external law (called *dharma*) and when we depart from the law then our *karma* is increased, and if we die with more *karma* than we had when we were born, then the next existence (or 'incarnation') will be less satisfactory than the present one has been. But if in this life I can keep within the *dharma*, then I shall die with less *karma* than I had when I was born, and so the next life will be better.

In fact in accountancy terms *karma* is like the 'balance carried forward' at the end of an account. But in Hindu thinking the balance is always a debit balance and the aim is to reduce the debit balance to zero. It never becomes a credit. But when an individual is able to reduce the debit balance to zero, then that individual can escape from the terrible cycle of birth and rebirth, the cycle of *samsara*.

So for the Hindu, life is not unfair. It is true that between the apparent boundaries of my birth and my death life does not appear to make sense. But the boundaries are imaginary. Life has no beginning and no end. Take all my lives and put them into one story and you will see that all through the story, in each rebirth, I get exactly what I deserve.

The problem with the Hindu answer is, of course, that it can't be tested. I can't remember my previous existences so I still don't know whether my present pains are a fair price to pay for my past sins. The other problem with the Hindu answer is that it tends to make people fatalistic. If your suffering is the proper price that you must pay for past sins then I don't help you by removing your suffering. If you don't suffer then you won't pay off the *karma* debt that you owe.

The caste system of Hinduism illustrates this very well. Everyone belongs to a caste, a particular level of society. Your caste is decided by your birth, and your birth is decided by the *karma* you brought with you from your previous life. If you are born an out-caste and your parents are out-castes (not part of the caste system), it is your own fault, and an out-caste you must remain, fated to perform only the most menial of tasks. It is striking that the caste system is so fixed in Hinduism that even Gandhi, with all his immense prestige, was unable to eliminate it, although he saw how unfair it is.

And then Hinduism tries to deal with present suffering by denying that it is real (the Christian Scientists take much the same line of argument). According to Hindu thinking the world consists of reality and illusion. Illusion is material. Illusion is bricks and tables and houses and flesh and blood. Reality is the eternal, the ultimate. The only bit of me that is real is the *karma* that I carry round. And that can't be destroyed by a bomb or hurt by a disease. In perhaps the most famous of the many Hindu sacred books, the *Bhagavad-Gita*, Arjuna, a young prince, is on the brink of a great civil war. The opposing armies are drawn up. And he can see, on both sides, friends of his, even relatives of his. And he doesn't see the sense of them killing one another for his sake:

> I do not long for victory O Krishna, nor kingdom nor pleasures . . . those for whose sake we desire kingdom, enjoyments and pleasures, they stand here in battle, renouncing their lives and riches, teachers, fathers, sons and also grandfathers, uncles. . . . These I would not consent to kill, though they kill me . . . only sin will accrue to us if we kill. . . . Why should we not have the wisdom to turn away from this sin, O Krishna?

So he appeals to the god Krishna, who is in one of his many incarnations as Arjuna's charioteer. But Krishna doesn't agree with Arjuna. All this talk about blood and death and suffering is unworthy of a prince. He should know that it is all *maya*, illusion. The only reality is the unseen which can never be hurt by a war:

> Whence has come to thee this stain of spirit in the hour of crisis? It is unknown to men of noble mind. . . . Yield not to this unmanliness O Arjuna. Cast off this petty faintheartedness. . . . Wise men do not grieve for the

dead or for the living. Never was there a time when I was not, nor thou, nor these lords of men, nor will there ever be a time hereafter when we all shall cease to be . . . the man who is not troubled by these, O Arjuna, who remains the same in pain and pleasure, who is wise, makes himself fit for eternal life. He who thinks that this slays, and he who thinks that this is slain; both of them fail to perceive the truth: this one neither slays nor is slain.[2]

And so the battle is fought until almost everyone on both sides is dead.

OTHER RELIGIOUS EXPLANATIONS

Islam offers a different explanation of suffering: ignorance. People do what they ought not to do, and reap the consequences. Muhammad came to remove their ignorance. In fact the period before Muhammad is called by Muslims *al-jahiliya*, the time of ignorance. Muhammad gave to Islam the Quran and the 'Traditions' (the *Hadith*), and from these two has come a law, the *Sharia*. Obedience to the law will produce harmony and end 'meaninglessness'. Islam denies that we cannot obey laws and denies any idea that we are 'fallen'. True enough we have a tendency towards doing wrong, but if we have the right law then we can and should obey it.

Again there is a second strand to the Muslim explanation: God has already written down the whole history of humanity. The history of the human race and with it the history of each individual is written there in the *Preserved Tablet* (the tablet on which, according to Islam, there is a record of the history of the world from which revelations have been given from God from time to time). All that is to happen to us is already decreed. It is for us to accept those decrees of good and of what we would call evil. We must submit to his mysterious plans. If there is an earthquake it is part of the inscrutable purpose of Allah, and it is not for us to respond that 'it isn't fair'. On the contrary we are to submit. That is the actual meaning of the word 'Islam': 'submission'.

African traditional religion offers a variation of this. Any kind of tragedy, whether on a personal or national level, is due to someone having offended the ancestors. The explanation would probably not involve the Creator God (sometimes called the 'High God' or the 'Sky God'), because he is so unimaginably great that he couldn't be expected to be affected by our activities. He is rather like the 'clock-maker god', who has built the clock, wound it up, and left it to run. But the ancestors (or sometimes the lesser gods or spirits) can be offended if we fail to perform our duty to them. And the answer to tragedy, therefore, is to find out what we have done wrong and to make amends: to offer some kind of sacrifice, perhaps.

THE GENESIS OF A CHRISTIAN EXPLANATION

Christianity has a very different answer to the problem of suffering.

What I am trying to do here is rather complicated. To begin with, I do not want to deny the reality of suffering, to pretend that it doesn't exist or that it isn't really bad. Also, I still want to hold on to my belief in a God of kindness and love, and compassion, a God who is fair and not arbitrary. Then I have to explain how such a God could produce such a painful world. And finally I have to explain why it is that God allows evil, why he permits murder and war. Why doesn't he intervene?

The Christian answer then is first of all that the world is not the way God intended it to be, and it is not the way that one day it will be. It is a *fallen* world. Secondly we reply that God is *not* omnipotent. It is not he who produces a painful world, but we. We go on to say that God has already intervened in the world in various ways, but most importantly in the coming of Jesus into the world, and that because of Jesus the process of putting the world straight has begun.

I have to face the fact that for many people the very idea of a real historical 'fall' is very difficult to accept. Perhaps memories of Sunday School or RE lessons or sermons have given us a perception of the traditional fall that almost forces us to put the fall into the same category as fairy stories. Well, let's look at it in a slightly different way. Supposing we set on one side the Bible's account of the fall, still it would be true that most of us would agree that it is fair to describe the world as 'fallen'. If it ever was even a good world, let alone a perfect world, it has certainly fallen a long way from that state.

Then it is still possible to see that the misery of the world is the result not of one particular fall, but of countless numbers of individual falls throughout history: people 'falling' from what intuitively they know is the right way to what they equally intuitively sense to be the wrong way. People falling repeatedly, until eventually they find it hard to tell right from wrong, until conscience is all but dead. And so little people commit little crimes and powerful people commit powerful crimes, little people commit murder, powerful people start wars and sell guns and bombs and tanks and missiles and even uranium for the manufacture of atomic bombs.

Actually the Christian response would be the same whichever model you choose to take. I don't particularly want to argue about history but I really want to start at a point on which we are all agreed: the world is a place of pain and fear and hopelessness for most people; we don't appear to be able to do much about it, but if there is a God out there then he should be able to do something about it. It is a fallen world that needs to be picked up again, a Humpty Dumpty world that needs to be put together again.

3
About God

The discreditable episode known as the Incarnation
C.S. Lewis, *The Screwtape Letters*

When we discuss God we usually think of him as being *omnipresent, omniscient, omnipotent*: you can't escape from God, he is everywhere; you can't hide anything from God, he knows everything; and you can't resist God, he can do anything.

The first point is neatly illustrated by Psalm 139:

> Whither shall I go from thy Spirit
> or whither shall I flee from thy presence?
> If I ascend to heaven, thou art there!
> If I make my bed in Sheol, thou art there!
> If I take the wings of the morning
> and dwell in the uttermost parts of the sea,
> even there thy hand shall lead me,
> and thy right hand shall hold me.
> If I say, 'Let only darkness cover me,
> and the light about me be night,'
> even the darkness is not dark to thee,
> the night is bright as the day;
> for darkness is as light with thee.

So God is omnipresent, he is everywhere, he can't be shut out.

But *omniscience* is more of a problem. Does God know everything? At first we are likely to say that he does, but I know and you know something that God will never know. I know what it's like to be wrong. I know what it's like to do something that's wrong. True enough we believe that Jesus

18

'carried our sins' (1 Pet. 2.24) and that he 'became sin for us' (2 Cor. 5.21), but no one who knew him ever accused him of actually sinning. So when we talk about God being omniscient, all-knowing, we don't quite mean what we say.

And when we come to the third word, *omnipotent*, we have an even bigger problem. Obviously God cannot do what is absurd: he can't turn three into an even number. He can't add five to six and get thirteen. He can't produce a square that is also a triangle. He can't make gobbledegook, nonsense words, into something meaningful. He can't make 'love' rhyme with 'hate', still less can he make 'love' mean the same as 'hate'. If he did that kind of thing then we would no longer be able to understand one another. Once we have human language there are certain regularities attached to it, and even God has to keep the regularities if he is going to speak the language.

God can't contradict his own nature. Since he has revealed himself in the Bible as a God of love and compassion and grace (as well as a God of justice, let's not forget) then he can't actually behave like a mass murderer. And if it is God who actually plans our wars then surely that's what he is: no longer a God of love but a mass murderer.

Islam says that Allah plans everything, including the wars and the famines. But Christianity is different: we dare to say that God is not in fact omnipotent, and that we are free to disobey God. Is God 'on the throne' as I sometimes hear evangelicals saying? In one sense, yes, he is. He created the world, and he knows where it is going: he knows the end of it all. But in another sense, no, he isn't on the throne. After all, Jesus himself taught us to pray 'Thy will be done on earth, as it is in heaven.' In other words, God's will is being done in heaven, but it is not yet being done here on earth, except to some limited extent. God's will is not being done in my life, except to some limited extent. Every time I argue with my wife I show that God's will is not being done on earth. And without doubt that's one of the least of my acts of disobedience.

Let us put the matter very bluntly. In England, in 1993, a small boy, James Bulger, was snatched away from his mother when they were out shopping. Two older boys grabbed him, took him away, horribly beat him and then murdered him. Did God plan that? Was God on the throne when that was being done? Everything inside me cries out 'No!' When in Rwanda twenty-one children and their thirteen Red Cross guardians were slaughtered, was God on the throne? Did God plan that? When the slag heap thundered down the mountain above Aberfan and engulfed the school, did God give the slag heap the push that started it all off?

The fact is that some Christian writers do preserve the omnipotence of God, they do keep God 'on the throne' even if it means that he wills these atrocities. Somehow it is hoped that there will be found a means of keeping a sovereign God who is also compassionate:

> Take, for instance, the Nazi persecution of the Jews. However perplexing it may be, it is an inescapable fact that God did not step in as the millions were driven into the gas chambers. God's inactivity creates a tremendous problem to those who believe he is in control, but at least they are convinced that his justice and wisdom and love will be finally vindicated.[1]

I cannot see that this naive hope could ever be justified.

When we say 'God is on the throne' we are using our emotions, but we aren't thinking. In Christianity we are prepared to recognise that if we are to be free, to choose, then in some sense we can (and we do) dethrone God. Even so we must recognise that while God's rule may be flouted here, and governments, armies, politicians, the rich, the powerful, may act in ways totally opposed to what we might expect him to will, those actions do not actually dethrone him. After all, the laws of this country are being broken every second of every day, but the Prime Minister is still there, the Queen is still the Queen. Sometimes the lawbreaker is caught and punished, sometimes not. In a perfect society the law-breaker would always be caught. And again there's the rub: if Christians have got it right God is not dethroned, and every law-breaker is eventually brought to book.

And this is what is meant by the *justice* of God. Clearly it is not a feature of this present world, but what if death is not the end, what if there is something beyond? What if in that world the injustice of this world is remedied? And what if not merely our sins against humanity and our high-handed rejection of God, but even our abuse of the world he made, our indifferent abuse of the animal kingdom, has to be answered for? That would be justice indeed!

In fact evangelical Christians confuse what should be with what actually is. It's not surprising that this confusion occurs because the New Testament frequently states what ought to be the case as though it were in fact the case. Paul wrote to the tumultuous Christians at Corinth that they were 'not lacking in any spiritual gift' (1 Cor. 1.7) and yet just a sentence or so later he is rebuking them because the church was filled with dissension, argument and division. Writing to the Christians at Ephesus he says that there is 'one body, and one Spirit . . . one hope . . . one Lord, one faith, one baptism, one God and Father of us all' (Eph. 4.4–6). Well, yes, theoretically that was true, but practically? Already Paul knew of divisions in the churches in Corinth and in Galatia. Writing to Colossae Paul announces confidently that Christ has 'disarmed the principalities and powers' (Col. 2.15) but he knew only too well their continuing might. There are great truths lying behind these statements, but they are not yet realised truths.

As yet God is not on the throne. His will is not yet done on earth, as it is in heaven.

This is a momentous statement. If God really is 'omnipotent', if he has already determined how we shall live, the very words we shall say, the decisions we think we are making, then God is responsible for the world and everything that happens in it. He is to blame. Consequently, I am not responsible and I am not to blame. God cannot put me in the dock, accused of wilful rebellion, because I never had a will. Instead judgment days becomes the day when God is judged and condemned by humanity. Of course, there can be no point in my trying to 'put things right' because from God's standpoint they are already right. This world is the way God planned it. If tomorrow is 'better' then that will be because God planned it to be better tomorrow, and not because of any decision I might have taken. I don't take decisions. I can't take decisions. God is on the throne.

THREE GODS OR ONE GOD?

I have some sympathy with both Muslims and Jews who see the Christian idea of the Trinity as being thinly disguised tri-theism. Even from inside Christianity and on the fringes of Christianity there has been fairly continuous opposition to trinitarian theology: the Unitarians are one group, Jehovah's Witnesses another. Our problem and the problem of the theologians has been in reconciling the New Testament account of Jesus, and then of the Spirit, with the Old Testament insistence on the one-ness of God. Christian theologians right through history have seen the problem, and have tried to find some way of expressing the paradox of 'three in one' and 'one in three' and frankly have failed. The paradox remains. But all orthodox Christians accept the paradox, and content themselves by saying that one would expect the nature of God to be rather more complex than our arithmetic tables.

If there is a problem in trinitarian theology it isn't all loss: there is an important gain, too. The most important gain is the incarnation, the belief that Jesus of Nazareth was not merely one more prophet in a long line of prophets stretching back through John the Baptist to Malachi and on back to Isaiah and Elijah, but that he was essentially different: he was God himself. Of course Hinduism finds no difficulty at all with such an idea, and can happily place Jesus among the many incarnations of god, including the one already referred to in an earlier chapter. But many of us feel uncomfortable with the idea of God incarnate, perhaps partly because we have been told that this notion, of the gods coming down to earth, is a very old notion indeed. Actually it isn't. Most such myths appear after this period of history, not before it.[2]

But given the Christian view of the Trinity there is a brilliant upside to the incarnation. The upside is more than the often limited view of 'salvation' associated with the crucifixion and resurrection and ascension of Jesus. The upside for me is that because of the incarnation God has got inside our time system, has actually experienced life as we know it, has been limited by time, has experienced the tension between what *could* be and what it actually *is* (one of John Macquarrie's four polarities discussed on p. 45 below), and has wrestled them into submission to him. Jesus lived the kind of life that we were always meant to live, and yet lived it from within our constraints. Christians have always insisted that the incarnation was real, not an elaborate charade. Jesus really was hungry, tired, thirsty and even ignorant. Because of the incarnation the second Person of the Holy Trinity, the one who is eternally Son of God, Jesus, like us, did not know the details of the end-time.

More than that: through his life Jesus actually experienced and accepted the apparent unfairness of life, its apparent meaninglessness. He *could* have done what we have done, and shouted to the world: 'It's not fair, life doesn't make sense.' And when finally he was crucified, his tormentors wrung from him the cry 'My God, why have you forsaken me?' – exactly what many a martyr must have cried in just such a situation.

In my time in Addis Ababa, Ethiopia, I had a Bible study group. All sorts of people came, among them the wife of the mayor. She was also a qualified nurse, and that is an essential part of my story. One evening, at the end of the group meeting, she asked me if I would follow her car home, to see that she arrived safely. The Marxist revolution was underway and she knew that she was on the list of people to be arrested; she wanted us to know when it happened. Well, she reached home safely that night. But next morning they came for her. Jember was in prison for eight years, for no better reason than that she was married to the mayor.

I next saw her twelve years later. The short-lived Marxist revolution was over, the prisoners were freed, and Jember came to England, to my home. She told us of her experiences. But most especially I recall her telling us of her third Christmas in prison. This was not a civilised prison, but a hell on earth; there were sometimes a dozen, sometimes as many as twenty women in a single room perhaps ten feet square. There were mattresses on the floor, no other furniture. Another Christmas, and her prayers for freedom still unanswered. She sat on the floor, her dejection, her tears, only too obvious. She was ready to shake her fist at God: 'It's not fair!' But one of the other prisoners came to her, asked her why she was so dejected. She wasn't usually that way. She replied, simply, honestly: 'It's just that – I don't know why I'm here . . ..' The woman looked at her with deep sympathy, and yet with some surprise, and I'll not forget her words to Sister Jember:

But that's our question, not your question. We don't know why we're here. But we know why you're here. When one of us is ill, who cares for us? You do! When one of us comes to childbirth, who looks after the mother and the baby, who knows what to do? You do! When one of us learns that her husband has been shot, who is it who gives comfort? You do! Oh yes! We know why you are here.

Jember didn't know, and she felt the unfairness of it all. Crucified, Jesus shared that sort of experience.

But there was this difference: Jesus was God. And Jesus took with him in his ascension that unique, that vital experience, the experience of undeserved suffering, and what it does to us when we experience it. He knows.

There is still more to this upside of the incarnation. Through the life of Jesus we are able to see in an understandable way what the character of God is. That's why through the centuries, although all sorts of accusations of hypocrisy and so on have been levelled at Christians and Christianity (which are often well deserved), there has been almost universal approval of Jesus. If God is like *this* then we like him. Jesus does not appear alongside the Prince Arjuna, but alongside the fisherman Peter; he is not shown in company with people of great integrity, but as the friend of prostitutes. He does not stand up for the rich and powerful, but for the poor and powerless. He does not blame, but shows an incredible grace and sensitivity. When a woman caught in the very act of adultery is dragged before him (we don't know what happened to the man) Jesus turns on her accusers and sends them away in shame, unforgiven, disgraced, while he sends the woman away forgiven!

Jesus sees the suffering of his world. Matthew 8 presents us with the suffering of a paralysed man, Peter's mother-in-law, and two violently disturbed men; while Matthew 9 shows us another paralysed man, the tax-collector Matthew, who sold his services to the Romans and was despised by his contemporaries, a grief-stricken father, whose daughter has just died, a woman with continual menstrual bleeding, two blind men and a dumb man. And the word that describes Jesus's attitude to every one of them is 'compassion'. We read that word (Matt. 9.36) and we respond: 'If this is God incarnate, I like him.'

Our frustration is that Jesus isn't here any more. He is rather like that faint, lingering, tantalising memory on awakening, the memory of a wonderful dream, but despite our every effort to hold on to it, to recapture it, it slips away. Jesus is no longer here.

AND THE HOLY SPIRIT?

Christianity has one further unique concept: if God, the mysterious triune God, is beyond our knowledge, and if we can only know about him through Jesus who is no longer with us, there is still a further hope – the Spirit.

I must pause for a moment here to point out that Christianity is unique in its idea of a Trinity. This is what is special about Christianity: it is not simply a restatement of other religions, not merely a variation on an old theme. Its theology is simply different. No-one would have dreamed it up. Could anyone have dreamed up a chosen nation, a succession (not just a class) of prophets related to a scheme of revelation? A chosen moment in time when God would stand on the earth and be lifted up from it on a cross? A triune God, one and yet three, three and yet one? And the third is the Spirit, the Holy Spirit. There is no religion with anything approaching this daring defiance of the many traditions of religions through the ages.

Some Christians seem to be embarrassed by this oddity, this failure to conform. But I cannot see why we should be embarrassed. Be embarrassed, rather, at a religion which is some mere variant of all the rest, and be embarrassed at claiming uniqueness for *that*. But surely we should exult in such an extraordinarily unique revelation as Christianity. As Professor Colin Gunton said in his 1992 Bampton Lectures, 'We could . . . make far more of the narrative peculiarities than we do, and glory rather more in the scandal of the one crucified for the sins of the world.'[3]

God is Father, Son and Spirit. The Spirit is to us what Jesus was to his first followers: Jesus taught them the truth, and the Spirit teaches us the truth. He gave them their orders, the Spirit gives us our orders. Jesus was the living Word, the Spirit inspired the written word. Jesus reassured his followers that they really were his people, and the Spirit does the same for us. The Spirit is not Jesus come back in ghostly form. Jesus was crucified for us, the Spirit was not. The Spirit came to the apostles at Pentecost, Jesus did not.

It does seem to me that this provision of the Spirit for this present time, present in some unique way with each Christian, is what makes it possible for Christians to cope with otherwise intolerable hardships. Princess Sophia Desta is a granddaughter of Emperor Haile Selassie of Ethiopia. When the Marxist revolution came to Ethiopia the royal family was rounded up, some, like Prince Iskinder, the Emperor's grandson, Commander of the Ethiopian navy, were shot, others simply imprisoned. 'Simply' imprisoned: after the comfortable lives they had lived it must have been appalling. There was nowhere to wash; the toilet was a hole in the ground; they were packed together in one room and denied access to the rest of the family, not for a week or so but year after year. It came to an end eventually. They were freed when the Marxist regime fell. Princess Sophia came to England, had nowhere to go, and so for several months lived with my wife and me in our home.

Among the students at London Bible College was an Iranian girl, whose family had been destroyed by the Khomeini regime, and she could not, would not forgive them. Sophia insisted on seeing her and talking to her; she begged and pleaded with her: you *must* forgive. She herself had been imprisoned for no offence other than being a member of the royal family. She had no trial, no sentence. She was insulted, starved, humiliated, but she forgave. Sophia was and is a Christian.

Of course the anecdote doesn't prove anything. Others have forgiven, too: Jews who have passed through the holocaust, come alive out of Auschwitz and Belsen, and have given up on hate. But for Christians the Spirit of Christ will not allow them to rest with a hating conscience, and leads them patiently, gently into the healing paths of forgiveness.

The Christian can unhesitatingly stand with the Jew and affirm in the words of the *Shema*, 'the Lord our God is one Lord', and can stand with the Muslim, and in the words of the *Kalima* say, 'There is no god but God'. And yet there is always this non-negotiable difference: Father, Son, Spirit.

A GOD OF COMPASSION

Now that we have got through the Christian idea of the Trinity I shall try to maintain a distinction between God, the triune God, and the three Persons of the Trinity, Father, Son and Spirit. So from here on 'God' means the triune God.

Jesus revealed the character of God by living among us, putting himself into the everyday experiences of humanity, experiencing the pains and hurts and tears of life, and then allowing us to see his response to each situation. He met people suffering from leprosy, people who were shunned by everyone else partly because it was thought that the disease was highly contagious, partly because it was thought to be an illness which was peculiarly used as a punishment by God. Jesus *touched* them. Jesus met that tragi-comic tax-collector Zacchaeus and invited himself to a meal in his home: good Jews didn't eat with quisling tax-collectors.

Jesus had several encounters with death. He was especially touched by the grief of the bereaved. My father was in the Royal Air Force and died in Malta just a few weeks after my twin brother and I were born. He was buried there, in Malta. A few years ago my brother and I went back to the island to try to find his grave. On the last day of our stay we stood by that grave, in a quiet, shady, beautifully kept military ceme-tery near to that haven of peace where the cars and buses of the tourists may not enter, the Silent City of Mdina. And as I stood there I was deeply troubled by my feelings. I wasn't sad, I was angry. It seemed such an inappropriate response, and not at all the response appropriate to a Christian. And then my thoughts went to St John's account of the death of Lazarus. When Jesus came to the grave Lazarus had already been dead four days. Jewish belief was that the spirit of the dead person hovered near the body for three days, and only then departed. Lazarus was dead. Jesus saw Mary crying, and her friends crying, and John says 'He was deeply moved in spirit'. Charles Kingsley Barrett, in one of the most sensitive of the many commentaries on John's Gospel, says that it is 'beyond question' that the word used here implies anger. At that grave Jesus was angry, not merely sad. Several sugges-tions have been made as to why he was angry: perhaps it was because of the unbelief of the mourners, or because the miracle which was forced on him would precipitate his death. Standing by that grave in Malta I sensed that I knew why Jesus was angry: he was aware of all that death robs us of. I was angry because my life might have been so different. True I had a stepfather, who was as kind as he felt able to be, but I never knew the love or the comradeship of a father. I never had a father to train me up in the way I should go, to rejoice when I did well, to rebuke when I did wrong. And I realised with something like excitement that my reaction was not wrong, that I was walking where Jesus had walked. Jesus was angered by the appalling results of a fallen humanity, angered by death, the most potent evidence of that fall. He was sorry for me, and the millions like me.

Unlike those hypocrites who dragged the adulterous woman before him, Jesus did not rejoice in evil. He did not thirst for punishment: 'I don't condemn you . . . go, but don't sin any more.'

Jesus showed God to be a God who loves. He even loved those who turned away from him. There was the rich man who couldn't take the road to heaven because he was so rich . . . and as he turned away from Jesus we're told that 'Jesus loved him'. John's Gospel is characterised by the tantalising references to 'the disciple whom Jesus loved', and it seems perverse not to accept the obvious conclusion that this was the author of the Gospel, John, who is never named otherwise in it, but who names himself in perpetual delight and astonishment: the disciple whom Jesus loved.

Jesus showed God to be the God of all compassion. Islam has it right: at the beginning of every chapter of the Quran except one (and that is probably because originally two chapters were joined together) the ascription appears: 'In the name of God the Compassionate, the Merciful' (in fact using two words that come from the same root). Matthew uses some of my favourite words from the New Testament: 'When Jesus saw the crowds he had compassion for them, because they were harassed and helpless, like sheep without a shepherd' (Matt. 9.36).

But all of this simply compounds our problem: how does a God of love and grace, mercy and compassion allow war and famine and earthquake, disease, rape and murder, when a mere word spoken out of his omnipotence would end it all?

4
God's World

Screwtape on God's relation to humanity:

All His talk about Love must be a disguise for something else – He must have some *real* motive for creating them and taking so much trouble about them. The reason one comes to talk as if He really had this impossible Love is our utter failure to find out that real motive. What does He stand to make out of them? That is the insoluble question.

C.S. Lewis, *The Screwtape Letters*

A CHAOTIC WORLD

God made the world and everything in it. Just how he brought that about we don't know. Scientists talk about some primeval 'big bang' from which came the universe as now we know it. Christians, Jews and Muslims all agree that God did it.

At the beginning of the Bible we have a picture of God inspecting the universe that he had made and 'it was very good'. We would expect that God, with his (almost) un-limited power, would create a world that was very good. We can often catch a glimpse of it: a beautiful spring morning, a holiday scene in the Mediterranean, the cloud-wreathed Mount Kinabalu in Malaysia, the stillness of Wastwater in England's Lake District, the majesty of the Grand Canyon.

But to be honest, no one looking at the world today would say 'it's very good'. Fighting in Africa, flooding in Asia, scandal in America, fear in Europe, and the resources that God in his goodness hid in the earth for us exploited, ravaged, ruined. The world as we see it today doesn't make much sense.

Billy . . . turned on the television. He came slightly un-
stuck in time, saw the late movie backwards. . . . It was a
movie about American bombers in the Second World War
and the gallant men who flew them. Seen backwards by
Billy, the story went like this:

American planes, full of holes and wounded men and
corpses took off backwards from an airfield in England.
Over France a few German fighter planes flew at them
backwards, sucked bullets and shell fragments from some
of the planes and crewmen. They did the same for
wrecked American planes on the ground, and those
planes flew up backwards to join the formation.

The formation flew backwards over a German city that
was in flames. The bombers opened their bomb bay
doors, exerted a miraculous magnetism which shrank the
fires, gathered them into cylindrical steel containers, and
lifted the containers into the bellies of the planes. The
containers were stored neatly in racks. The Germans below had miraculous devices of their own, which were long
steel tubes. They used them to suck more fragments
from the crewmen and the planes. But there were still a
few wounded Americans, though, and some of the
bombers were in bad repair. Over France, though, German fighters came up again, made everything and every-
body as good as new.

When the bombers got back to their base, the steel
cylinders were taken from the racks and shipped back
to the United States of America, where factories were
operating night and day, dismantling the cylinders,
separating the dangerous contents into minerals.
Touchingly it was mainly women who did this work.
The minerals were then shipped to specialists in re-
mote areas. It was their business to put them into the
ground, to hide them cleverly, so they would never
hurt anybody ever again.

(Kurt Vonnegut, Slaughterhouse Five)

Actually the world makes more sense seen backwards.

AN ORDERED WORLD

What kind of world has God made? Above all it's a world of regularities: it is held together by laws. There are the laws which govern electricity, the law of gravity, and the laws which govern the ways in which different elements combine to give new substances. There's the extraordinary law which takes two gases, oxygen and hydrogen, and lays it down that when they are combined under proper conditions they will produce water. Or to be frivolous, there are the laws that allow a brown cow eating green grass under a blue sky to produce white milk.

We take these regularities for granted, but we can't *know* that the laws which were discovered yesterday will still be true tomorrow. But if it were not so, life would be impossible. We couldn't turn on a light switch with any confidence: anything might happen. In fact we know that 'anything' can't happen because we have a world of regularities.

A 'FALLEN' WORLD

Then we have a fallen world. I have already indicated that I don't much mind how you deal with the idea of a fall; nor do I much mind how you interpret the third chapter of Genesis, the first book in the Bible but it's a very important chapter. It expresses a certainty that something has gone badly wrong with this world. Some people treat the opening chapters of Genesis as literal history. According to this view, there was a real Adam and a real rib was taken from his side and from it God formed a woman. There was a real garden of Eden and Adam and Eve lived in it, and in the evenings God came down to talk to them. There was a real snake that could stand up straight and could talk.

Other people say that this is nothing more than another folk tale, similar to many found in African traditional religions, telling how God was driven away from humankind. According to some tales this was because the women chattered so much and made God's head ache; in others it was because the pounding of the women's big pestles in their wooden mortars as they ground up the grain meant that God couldn't get to sleep.

Still others point to the last book in the Bible, which introduces a 'great red dragon'. This is eventually identified as 'that ancient serpent, who is called the Devil and Satan, the deceiver of the whole world', an obvious reference back to Genesis 3. It is argued that since Revelation 12 is certainly not meant to be taken literally but as an allegory, we should do the same with Genesis 3.

Whichever way you take it Genesis 3 is there to make an important point: this world is a fallen world. Something has gone wrong with it, it is not the way God meant it to be. And it is not God's fault, but ours.

But I feel that I must deal with this question of how to understand these opening chapters of Genesis because they seem to be such a problem for so many people. They are a problem for people who take the chapters as simple literal history. A day is a day with twenty-four hours in it. A serpent is a snake, just like the snakes we have around today. And it spoke. There are problems in these chapters even for earnest believers in the literal interpretation. There is all the scientific evidence that consistently and uncompromisingly points to a very different scenario: humanity is much much older than the Genesis account, taken literally, suggests; some kind of evolution has undoubtedly occurred. To deny it is to place oneself in a minority of one, and, worse, to close one's eyes to unpalatable facts. But that blindness might be acceptable: one simply insists that everyone else is out of step, out of faith, and it is they who are blinded by science. But there are other problems. The creation story in Genesis 1 speaks of morning and evening for day one and yet the sun, moon and stars don't appear until day four. How can one have literal days without the sun? Indeed how can one have planet earth without the sun around which it traces its planetary orbit?

I have to say that I see the early chapters of Genesis not as a scientific account of the mechanism of creation, but as a vital, fundamental prologue to theology. It is there to make fundamental, vital, distinctive, even unique claims about this universe. The first of these statements is that the world is not merely a cosmic accident: God created it. The second is that humanity, in its turn, is not a mere cosmic accident but created by God; human beings are the climax of creation. Thirdly, humanity has always had freedom to choose between right and wrong, between good and evil, between obedience and disobedience, between dependence on the Creator and proud independence. These are the crucial foundations of all biblical theology.

Exactly how this happened is for science to tell us. It will probably never get it quite right. I started out as a scientist, studying physics. That was forty years ago. In our first two years we studied classical physics. In our third year we were told: 'Now you can forget all that', and we were introduced to a different world of quantum and wave and probabilities. But almost all that I learned even in that third year is now known to be either actually wrong or at least inadequate. There is no reason to suppose that today's quarks, which were not even imagined in my day, and today's theories will be any longer lasting than yesterday's. Yet I am confident that with each passing year the scientists are getting closer to the truth. But, if I can be mathematical, their results take them along a line which is an asymptote to reality: it gets ever closer to reality, but will never reach it. This is my understanding of the opening chapters of Genesis and the supposed conflict with science. And I think that I ought to add that most scientists and philosophers who are evangelical Christians would agree with what I have suggested above.

A STRUCTURED WORLD

We also have a structured world, a tiered world which has several layers to it. At the lower end we have the inanimate world of water, soil, rocks, hills, deserts, mountains. Above that begins the living world, the world of tiny plants, green grass, bushes, and great trees. Above that again is the world of animal life, birds, fish. And this is where religion steps in: above all *that* is humanity, the peak of all that has been created. Psalm 8 expresses this idea very clearly:

> When I look at thy heavens, the work of thy fingers,
> the moon and the stars which thou hast established;
> what is man that thou art mindful of him,
> and the son of man that thou dost care for him?
> Yet thou hast made him little less than God,
> and dost crown him with glory and honour.
> Thou hast given him dominion over the works of thy
> hands;
> thou hast put all things under his feet,
> all sheep and oxen,
> and also the beasts of the field,
> the birds of the air, and the fish of the sea,
> whatever passes along the paths of the sea.

The song is interesting because it guards against worshipping humanity by enclosing the whole song of praise to *humanity* by a sentence ascribing praise to *God*:

> O Lord, our Lord,
> how majestic is thy name in all the earth!

And that takes us directly to the top level of the universe, that unique level where our faith places God, who brought all the rest into existence. He is distinguished from everything else: he is the Creator, all else is the created.

But according to Christianity there is a further tier between God and us, the spirit world, sometimes referred to in the Bible as 'angels' (which is actually a simple transliteration of the Greek word *angelos*). The Greek word used in the New Testament and the corresponding Hebrew word used in the Old Testament both mean 'messenger': whatever angels may be and however they may appear, they are messengers. The *angelos* may be human: John is called the

35

'angel' messenger of God (Matt. 11.10); the *angelos* may be from Satan, a Satanic messenger (2 Cor. 12.7). And this is where Christianity is very clear, but different from other religions: the spirit world, also, is a fallen world. It is a divided world. The messengers are, some of them, messengers of God. And some messengers are part of the fallen universe, and form a second force in the universe. In fact the account of the fall in Genesis 3, as it is interpreted in Revelation 12 (and we've discussed the relationship between them above, on page 33), suggests that however the *human* fall actually occurred, it was just one consequence of an already fallen *spirit* world.

A DIVIDED UNIVERSE

And that leads to a further point about creation: it is a divided creation, a creation containing two kingdoms. One is the kingdom of God; the second kingdom is the fallen kingdom. Jesus himself referred to this kingdom. He had been praying, teaching his followers to pray, and then he encountered a man who was dumb. He healed him. Jesus saw that healing as an attack on the second kingdom: 'Every kingdom divided against itself is laid waste, and a divided household falls. And if Satan also is divided against himself, how will his kingdom stand? . . . But if it is by the finger of God that I cast out demons, then the kingdom of God has come upon you' (Luke 11.17–18, 20). For Christianity the world is a complex world, and the spirit world, like us, is free to choose right or wrong. For Christianity the world is a fallen world, because part of the spirit world and part of the human world has used its freedom to turn against God.

Now it may seem asking a great deal to expect people in the twenty-first century to believe in a spirit world. But surely people who can believe in radio and television, computers and telephones, atoms and quarks, and in the vagaries, the peculiarities, and the absurdities of the sub-nuclear world should not really find it difficult to believe in a whole cosmos that while it is invisible to us nevertheless interacts with us.

I suppose the problem is that we have actually constructed an unbelievable model of what this other spiritual world is supposed to be, and since we can't believe in that, we can't believe in the reality it is supposed to represent. Much as C.S. Lewis pointed out in his *Screwtape Letters*: we picture the devil in red tights, with horns and a forked tail, and since we can't believe that, we blithely dismiss the devil. Perhaps we do need to demythologise the pictures and invite today's generation to use today's imagery (the devil as a computer virus!).

It does seem strange to me that fifty years ago when people perceived this to be a wholly materialistic world, people had a strong belief in Jesus, as example, great teacher, humanitarian, even prophet, but found it difficult to believe in God. But it seems now that people find it hard to believe in Jesus as a real historical figure, but have returned to their belief in God. I suspect that the expanding Christmas industry has a great deal to do with this odd state of affairs. We now have the Christmas story so confused that we adults have simply decided that none of it is true, although all of it is lovely. The wise men with their gifts of gold and incense and myrrh are confused with Father Christmas and his sack of toys. The Barbie doll under the Christmas tree is confused with Jesus in a manger. The choir of angels (that word again!) is confused with *Songs of Praise* and Rudolf the Red Nosed Reindeer flies through the Oxford Street lights, on to Bethlehem.

And just sometimes we pause to ask, wistfully, with John Betjeman:

And is it true? And is it true,
    This most tremendous tale of all,
Seen in a stained-glass window's hue,
    A Baby in an ox's stall?
The Maker of the stars and sea
Become a Child on earth for me?

And is it true? For if it is,
    No loving fingers tying strings
Around those tissued fripperies,
    The sweet and silly Christmas things,
Bath salts and inexpensive scent
And hideous tie so kindly meant,

No love that in a family dwells,
    No carolling in frosty air,
Nor all the steeple-shaking bells
    Can with this simple truth compare –
That God was Man in Palestine
And lives today in Bread and Wine.[1]

Hidden behind the Christmas absurdities is what Christians believe to be the most significant event in history. To rewrite a contemporary piece of dogma, the greatest event in history is not that man stood on the moon, but that God stood on the earth: Christ, here. Bringing together what were previously two separated worlds, the world of the divine and the world of humanity, the ultimate 'them and us'. At that point in history they came together, and came together for a purpose. The purpose was to begin the process of reconciling humanity to its Maker: to begin the process of restoring true humanity, to make it possible for us to be not only what we were always meant to be, truly human, but also what, deep down inside us, we have all, at some time, longed to be. And that meant, in theological terms, setting us free from the second, fallen, kingdom.

TIME AND THE OMNIPOTENT GOD

There is one more statement to make about the world: it is a world set in time. Our lives are dominated by time: yesterday, today, tomorrow, next week, next year. We keep diaries, make appointments, write histories. We get up in the morning, work through the day, relax in the evening, go to bed and then get up to another morning. We are taught that

there are sixty seconds to the minute and sixty minutes to
the hour and that twenty-four hours constitute a day.

While that is all scientifically true we know that some
minutes take longer to pass than other minutes. I am a
coward in the dentist's chair, and five minutes in that chair
are equivalent to an hour in most other places. Holidays
pass quickly, working days pass slowly. But still we know
the reality of time, the succession of past, present and
future.

Yet we also have some concept of eternity. In the Bible
'the Preacher' says of God that he has 'made everything
beautiful in its time; also he has put eternity into man's
mind, yet so that he cannot find out what God has done
from the beginning to the end' (Ecclus. 3.11). In some
sense eternity is where God is, and time is where we are.
The really significant difference between the two is that
God is on the throne in eternity, but he is not on the throne
here in time.

Jesus himself taught his people to pray: 'Thy kingdom
come, thy will be done on earth, as it is in heaven' (Matt.
6.10). His will *is* done in heaven, in eternity, and we pray
that it might similarly be done here on earth, in time. It
isn't, but we wish that it were, then the great tragedies of
world wars and massacres simply would not happen. And so
we come back to this notion of the sovereignty, the omnipotence, of God.

This distinction between time and eternity is important.
It helps us to correct our perception of God's omnipotence.
We have to admit that if what we see going on in the world
is God's will then he is a strange god, and not the God of the
Bible. And so we have argued that in some sense he is not
omnipotent. And that in turn had us worried, because it
seems rather a paradox to have God who is not on the
throne. But now we can see that in eternity he is on the
throne. Or to put it another way, the world is not out of
control after all. In his eternity God created time and God
created us and gave us freedom to choose; that, inside time,
limited his rule, his omnipotence. But the world was created

with a particular purpose in God's mind, and a particular programme in view. The purpose is the creation of a freely loving and worshipping community. That's exactly what we find at the end of the Bible, in John's vision of heaven. Within time human history takes many twists and turns, and human choice leads to tragic events. But in eternity the end is certain, the programme is fixed. We will return to this in chapter six, after we have looked at the human condition.

5
Humanity

The Irresistible and the Indisputable are the two weapons which the very nature of God's scheme forbids him to use.

C.S. Lewis, *The Screwtape Letters*

GOD MADE US LIKE HIMSELF

We have taken a very brief look at some ideas of God and his omnipresence, omniscience and omnipotence. We have looked at this complex world. Now we move on to consider humanity.

The first thing to be said is that God made us. Just how he made us is less important than the fact that we are not just a cosmic accident, a freak of evolution. God made us, and the writer of Genesis has God saying that he would make us in his image. It is that which distinguishes us from the rest of living creation.

This does not mean that, like us, God has a head made largely of bone, a liver, a pancreas, and so on. In his eternity there is no need for a liver and a pancreas, although it is understandably difficult for writers to speak of God other than in human terms. We do talk about his hands and his eyes, although not, I think, his pancreas. We do it because otherwise we wouldn't be able to say anything about him at all. He just becomes a mystery.

But worse. If we become too clever and refuse to speak about God as though he were a kind of superman (we use the term *anthropomorphic* to describe talking of God as though he were a man) then we may create for ourselves a quite absurd mental picture of God. I think that it was C.S. Lewis who admitted that he had tried to get rid of any image of God that was in any sense like a human being, and found to his horror that his mental picture of God ended up as a kind of extended celestial tapioca pudding: and what was worse, he admitted, he didn't *like* tapioca pudding.

God isn't like us in the material sense and we are not like him in terms of livers and the rest; but we are like him in a much more profound sense: we are morally free people. We can choose.

THE RIGHT TO CHOOSE

I am quite aware of the discussions that have gone on among philosophers about the reality or otherwise of free will. The argument doesn't take us anywhere at all: indeed it is arguable that if we have no free will and everything is determined, there is no point in arguing. The outcome of the argument also is predetermined. And where could anyone go from there?

There is a wonderful anecdote told of Andrade and Huxley, two of the great scientists and freethinkers of the nineteenth century who were arguing with one another in the dining room of a London hotel. Eventually they had argued themselves to a standstill. Huxley said: 'It's no good going on arguing. I know exactly what you're going to say next, I know exactly what you're going to do next.' Without saying a word Andrade got up from his chair, walked to the middle of the room and solemnly stood on his head. He returned to their table: 'That is to show you that you do *not* know what I am going to do next.'

The argument sometimes used by scientists who should know better is that if we knew the present state of every constituent molecule, atom, electron, muon, pion, quark, or whatever in all the universe, we could then infallibly predict the future state of the universe. It is true that we cannot as yet know the state of all these particles, but still, in principle we could, and thus in principle, and for all practical purposes, the future is determined. The fact is, of course, that the argument fails crucially: even in principle we cannot know the present state even of one particle. The state of any fundamental particle must be denoted statistically, not absolutely, and its future state is similarly a matter of statistical probability, not of formulaic certainty.

Of course it must at once be conceded that our freedom of choice is limited, circumscribed by our particular condition in life, the education we have, the money that allows us to accept the consequences of particular choices, the human relationships that effectively exclude some choices. But although we have limited choice, we still have choice. It seems to be of the essence of humanity that we may choose, and choose rationally. Not only so, but unlike the animals around us we may choose with a fair idea of the consequences likely to follow from that choice. And that awareness of probable consequences in turn arises from our understanding of the regularities which govern the universe. We know a great deal about electric currents, electrostatic fields, photo-electricity, radioactivity, photosynthesis, the function of the blood, the reason for the pancreas, the structure of space, the effect of gravity. And all this knowledge provides us with a predictable universe within which to make our decisions. Usually we make rational decisions but sometimes, as the philosopher-theologian John Macquarrie has pointed out, they are irrational.

That in turn explains the problem of requiring some ultimately powerful Absolute to intervene when we make a mistake. We all make mistakes. If the Almighty were to intervene each time we made a mistake two things would follow: we would lose this essential humanity of ours, this right to choose; and we would lose a predictable universe. It would at least appear to us as capricious: under certain unspecified conditions matches would not strike, lights would not go on, the car's accelerator would not work, gravity would be suspended.

That God, the Absolute, does intervene on occasion I cannot doubt. The reason why he does not do so with any regularity is rather obvious.

WE ARE BODY PLUS

Here, though, is something we cannot prove: that we are anything more than a material body. I remember as a very young and immature Christian reading somewhere of a very simple experiment which claimed to prove that we are body plus. They had placed a dying man on some scales, and then monitored his weight as he died. And at the moment of death suddenly his weight dropped! Something had left that body! It was so wonderfully simple, and so totally convincing. I still mentally blush when I think of myself confidently trading this story around as proof that we are body plus. Of course the experiment itself is wishful thinking, but the concept lying behind it is grotesque: that the plus bit is some kind of miniature me which flies away at death. A moment's thought should have told me that no scales ever invented could detect the departure of a *spirit*.

Yet I believe that I am body plus. I am not my finger, nor my feet, nor my head, nor my brain. Parts of each of them can be excised and I will still be me. But there is that of me which disciplines, or fails to discipline, my body, which makes it do what I will it to do, or which allows it to do what I do not want it to do. I know from almost daily experience what it is to debate with myself, not with my two feet or with one eye, but with myself, to argue with myself about what to do, where to go. I know what it is to make decisions to take actions that I also know to be contrary to my own best interests. They may be big things or small things: to give away my bar of chocolate to a child or go to the rescue of someone who is drowning.

Back in 1976, when I was still a missionary in Ethiopia, and when civil war between Ethiopia and Eritrea was still tearing the land apart, I heard that an Eritrean pastor had been kidnapped. I volunteered to fly up to Asmara to attempt to get him back from the Eritrean guerrillas. I didn't have to go. No one asked me to go. It was dangerous to go, but I went. And we all take decisions like that, decisions that appear to have no evolutionary survival value. Such decisions argue for a spirit.

THE POLARITIES OF HUMAN EXISTENCE

I have already suggested that there are limits to our freedom of choice. John Macquarrie, a very fine theologian, sees humanity as caught up in a network of opposites, with the opposites held in tension. He calls them *polarities*. He describes four of them, but we could readily identify more. He describes the polarity of possibility and facticity: what is theoretically *possible*, but what I know *in fact* is likely to happen. It is clearly possible, at present, to ensure that everyone in this world has enough to eat. To make that possibility into a reality would require many of us to eat less, many of our multinational corporations to make less profit, governments to co-operate. Practically I know and you know that all this is asking too much. Tonight, tomorrow night, and, apparently, for the foreseeable future, part of the world's population will go to bed taking indigestion pills to deal with gross overeating, while another part will not have a bed to go to and will probably not get much sleep, because they are hungry. These are the polarities of possibility and facticity.

I have already made reference to the polarity of rationality and irrationality. On the whole, perhaps, we tend to behave rationally, but here I hesitate. What is rational to you may not appear so to me, and both my behaviour and yours may appear irrational to God. I read in my newspaper that England's cricket captain, having totally unexpectedly won a test match in Australia, was asked how he planned to spend the next few days. Apparently the first thing he was going to do was to get drunk. To him it was, apparently, rational. More seriously we may well act irrationally at some point in our lives, risking our own well-being for the sake of someone else, or behaving destructively out of sheer frustration: a long period of unemployment, for example. We know quite well that smashing a window or two won't resolve the problem, but irrationally, that's what I might mean to do.

The third polarity is that between community and individuality. We are essentially, naturally, gregarious. It is normal for human beings to live together, work together, play together. We are born into a family, marry and have our own family, and probably also work in some kind of team relationship. In fact we are naturally suspicious of the individual who is a loner: such people are not normal. And yet we know that all these relationships inhibit our freedom. Alone I can please myself how I spend my days, but in a family or with a job, someone else has a claim on me. But the upside is that together with others I can do things, make things, and enjoy things that are impossible if I hold on to my individuality. Try playing tennis alone!

And the downside? We all know the downside. The children make enormous inroads into our 'free' time. One's husband or wife must be taken into account when planning holidays, housing, and even meals. Working for myself and by myself I can take a break for tea when I want to. When I work with others I have to take my tea break when everyone else does, or when no one else does. On my own I can practise playing the trombone at any time and at any volume, but not if I have neighbours.

The fourth polarity is the polarity of responsibility and impotence. We feel in some way responsible for the people having their homes destroyed in the fighting in Chechnya, in Bosnia, in Liberia, in Somalia. We feel that we want to do something about it, but we can't, we're impotent. Every time we hear about starving people we feel guilty about our own excellent meals. In some way we feel responsible for their problems, and therefore responsible for putting things right, yet we know that we can't do anything. There actually is plenty of food to feed everyone, but it's not distributed properly. And we can't see how to ensure that it is distributed the right way.

Now these polarities are in some sense inevitable. They are the consequence of being human. But they seem to form a net, a pattern of strings connected to one another, all under tension, pulling us this way and that: 'I ought to but I can't . . . I enjoy having people at the house, but I wish they knew when to leave . . . but it's no good feeling guilty, because there's nothing I can do about it. . . . I'm so confused . . . I wish I knew what to do. . . .'

TO BE TRULY HUMAN

Even if we have never tried to express our situation in terms of polarities we have known them all only too well. We are dissatisfied with life as it is, and we feel that it ought to be different, but we can't see any way of making it satisfactorily different. What we want is to be truly human. But those polarities are not merely inevitable, inescapable. They can actually be used constructively. I need both my solitariness and my togetherness. I need to feel responsible, but I also need to know what I can do and what I can't do; otherwise what I can't do will so overwhelm me that I won't do what I could do. There is a potential in those apparently destructive polarities that should be realised in our lives. In fact those polarities seem to serve only to prevent us from being truly human.

Let me explain that phrase. When I lived on the outskirts of Addis Ababa, the road from the villages out to the west ran not too far from my house. Along that road each day, there passed a long procession of women, bent over, loaded down with great bundles of sticks, gathered from the forests. They were taking them to the market to be sold. When they had sold their loads they walked back home, along that same dusty road. The next day was spent out in the forests, collecting wood. And the day after that they were back on the road near my house, to sell the firewood. And then they went back home and so on.

That was life. It began when they were about twenty-five years old. By the age of thirty-five they were old women. By forty most of them would be dead.

That's not human. I never got used to it, perhaps because I projected onto those trudging figures the image of my mother. I saw *her* loaded down with firewood, on that unending road of drudgery. It was degrading, wicked, inhuman. Theirs was not human living.

So what does it mean to be truly human? Well, first of all it means adjusting to those inescapable polarities so that their potential is realised. Put more simply, it means being truly me. According to Christian thinking every individual, every one of the six million Jews who died in the holocaust, every autistic child, every victim of a road accident, is a unique, irreplaceable human being. There has never in the whole history of the world been anyone else quite like you, and there never will be again. And that is what makes each of us so valuable. We aren't just statistics. We don't exist for the sake of society. We are irreplaceable, invaluable, individual.

To be truly human I need to be stable. That means not being pushed around by circumstances, not being forced to act a part, perhaps hypocritically, to try to appear what I am not, just to please everyone else. Shakespeare was right, though probably he didn't appreciate how philosophical he was being, when he said 'All the world's a stage, and all the people on it merely players.' Well, I don't want to be an actor. I want to stop play acting and to be me.

Then, although I want to be true to myself, I also want to be properly related to the community of which I am a part: my family, the people I work with, my neighbours. My human relationships are all *dyadic*: they all involve two people, me and one other. The problem here is that for each individual to whom I must relate there exist two *dyadic* relationships: how I relate to her and how she relates to me. As we all know only too well, it doesn't take two to make a quarrel: it only takes one. So if *her* attitude to me is a bad one then, even though my attitude to her is a good one, our relationship is under tension. The most I can do for these two dyadic relationships (affecting just one other person) is to ensure that one dyad is balanced and that my half of the second dyad is as balanced as it can be. Now see how that works out in the hundreds of dyadic relationships which together constitute my network of human relationships.

What I need is to have my uniqueness freed and expressed. And my relationships need to be released from their destructive tensions. Then I shall be able to live humanly productively and yet within the inescapable polarities of my existence. That appears to require a salvation, a deliverance, that is personal to me, affecting my community and my lifestyle. And that appears to require outside help. Something more than the habitual new year resolution.

In fact what I need is to be saved. Pope John Paul II was asked to clarify this generally misunderstood term and in his book *Crossing the Threshold of Hope* he replied:

> To save means to liberate from evil. This does not refer only to social evils, such as injustice, coercion, exploitation. Nor does it refer only to disease, catastrophes, natural cataclysms, and everything that has been considered disaster in the history of humanity.

> To save means to liberate from radical, ultimate evil. Death itself is no longer that kind of evil, if followed by the Resurrection. And the Resurrection comes about through the work of Christ. Through the work of the Redeemer death ceases to be an ultimate evil; it becomes subject to the power of life.

> The world does not have such power. The world, which is capable of perfecting therapeutic techniques in various fields, does not have the power to liberate man from death. And therefore the world cannot be a source of salvation for man. Only God saves.

6
Bringing the Two Together

> It is no doubt impossible to prevent his praying for his mother, but we have means of rendering the prayers innocuous. Make sure that they are always very 'spiritual', that he is always concerned with the state of her soul and never with her rheumatism.
>
> C.S. Lewis, *The Screwtape Letters*

We have looked at humanity and at the Christian understanding of God. Now we bring the two together; and oddly enough they are usually brought together by rheumatism and toothache rather than by a summer's day and good health. At least that appears to be the case for those who are uncertain about the existence of God. They turn to him when they need him.

I simply can't recall how many times I've met this strange urge of otherwise apparently irreligious people to pray. Suddenly helpless they cry out to a God in whom they have never really believed: 'Now I need him and I have nowhere else to go.' Abraham Lincoln confessed: 'I have been driven many times to my knees by the overwhelming conviction that I had nowhere else to go.' And yet that's a poor notion of prayer: to call on God when you need him and then when he has worked the trick, dealt with the problem, to go back to normal living, back to independence.

Contrast that with Harry Emerson Fosdick's insight into true prayer. He describes prayer as it is understood by the Sufis, the Muslim charismatics: 'There are three degrees in prayer. The first is when it is spoken only by the lips. The second is when, with difficulty, by a resolute effort, the soul succeeds in fixing its thought on divine things. The third is when the soul finds it hard to turn away from God.'[1] But few of us ever get beyond the shopping list view of prayer. As one Baptist minister once expressed it, this is 'putting all your begs into one ask-it'.

The difficulty is to find someone who knows how to work the trick, how to persuade God to do what I want him to do, to say yes to my 'ask-it'. And this is a problem not only for the essentially irreligious, but also for the committed Christian. The fact is that most ask-its don't bring the desired results.

One answer that is frequently given to the problem of suffering and illness in the world is prayer. By prayer we can bring order back into the world. By prayer we can recruit an omnipotent God into our ranks and persuade him to put everything right. If there is illness then prayer can banish it. If money is needed the prayer of faith will produce it. For the unemployed prayer is the answer: pray for a job, pray hard enough, with faith enough, and with enough people joining in the 'amen' at the end and God will provide the job. The problem is that he doesn't. A beautiful theory is slain by an ugly fact.

Now I have just one necessary comment for Christian readers: I'm not going to use the common rationalisation for unanswered prayer that 'It was answered, *really*. It just didn't get answered quite the way we mere mortals would expect.' I was once caring for a Baptist church in London when they had no minister. One of the church members had been ill with cancer, had been prayed for, and had recovered. The doctors would probably have called it remission, but she seemed to be well. And then the cancer returned. Some of her friends prayed for her healing: that was their ask-it. But only a week later she died. They told the rest of us that their prayers had been answered, *really*, because now she was completely healed. Well, so she was, but that was not what they had asked for. They had wanted her alive, well, and here. But they didn't get what they asked for.

I would rather be quite clear: many things we pray for we simply do not get.

UNANSWERED PRAYER

Even in the Bible we have some striking examples of un-answered prayer. Paul prayed that he would be delivered from some unspecified weakness (2 Cor. 12.7–9). Poetically he describes it as 'a thorn in the flesh, a messenger of Satan' and whatever it was he didn't like it. So he prayed for deliverance, and he didn't get it. Persevering he prayed twice more, and still he didn't get delivered. If it was an illness he was still ill. If it was harassment by some enemy, then he was still harassed. If it was some specific tempta-tion, he was still tempted. In any event his prayer wasn't answered.

Paul again at the end of his letter to Rome: 'I appeal to you, brethren, by our Lord Jesus Christ and by the love of the Spirit [see how important, how urgent he makes this appeal], to strive together with me [urgency again] in your prayers to God on my behalf, that I may be delivered from the unbelievers in Judea . . . so that by God's will I may come to you with joy and be refreshed in your company' (Rom. 15.30–32). And in Acts 28 we have Paul at last arriv-ing in Rome, having survived a riot and an attempted as-sassination in Jerusalem, a shipwreck and near legal murder on the way to Rome, and the bite of a poisonous snake in Malta! It wasn't a very obvious answer to prayer. True enough he got to Rome, and he met up with the Christians there: 'On seeing them Paul thanked God and took cour-age' (Acts 28.15). But two years of imprisonment lay ahead of him.

In Luke 22 we find Jesus asking that 'this cup' might be taken away. He did not want to drink it. The drink repres-ented an experience that he didn't *want* – the cross: 'Father, if it's possible, find some other way.' Like us in so many of our hard experiences it simply wasn't possible for Jesus to *want* the hard way, in his case to go to the cross.

Jesus added to his prayer a very significant footnote: 'Nevertheless, not my will, but thine, be done.' This beau-tifully illustrates both the problem of ask-its and the proper answer. The problem clearly lies in the existence of two wills: mine and his. And of course his will is going to be done. So if my ask-it is something that is not in his will then I am not going to get it. And then comes conflict unless I am prepared to echo the words of Jesus, 'Not my will, but yours'.

FOUR REASONS WHY OUR PRAYERS AREN'T ANSWERED

1. The first reason we have already seen: we don't have our prayer answered because *we are asking for something contrary to God's will*. God wanted and could use a weak Paul, but he couldn't use a strong Paul, so it was useless for Paul to be asking God to make him strong. As Paul discovered, there is a wonderful paradox in the Christian life: 'When I am weak, then I am strong.'

Again it was in God's will that Jesus should 'drink the cup', go to the cross. The prayer of Jesus that if it were possible some other way should be found was entirely proper, but it was vital that he should add the 'nevertheless'.

2. *Because our motives are wrong*: we are asking for something which would not be good for us. The classic explanation comes from James 4.3: 'You ask and do not receive, because you ask wrongly, to spend it on your passions.' James is writing about the state of the church, which was in some respects not much different from the state of the rest of society: he talks about 'friendship with the world'. The problem was that the Christians had exactly the same expectations, ambitions and desires as everyone else, and their prayers reflected that situation. What they prayed for anyone might pray for: pleasure. In fact the Greek word James uses is the word from which we get our word hedonism.

Now this could easily be misunderstood: many Christians are scared of pleasure, and particularly scared of sexual pleasure. Perversely they are only happy when they are

miserable. Now there's nothing inherently wrong in pleasure. C.S. Lewis has Screwtape explaining to the junior
tempter Wormwood the nature of God: 'He's a hedonist at
heart!' But there is something wrong with being obsessed
by it, by making pleasure our primary concern. Screwtape
has this to say:

> I know we have won many a soul through pleasure. All
> the same, it is His invention, not ours. He made the
> pleasures; all our research so far has not enabled us to
> produce one. All we can do is to encourage the humans to
> take the pleasures which our Enemy has produced at
> times, or in ways, or in degrees, which He has forbidden.[2]

That was the point being made by James. His answer was
simple: 'Submit yourselves, therefore, to God' (4.7). In
other words, *ask* him what is best for you in your situation:
don't *tell* him.

3. *Because of the quality of our request.* This problem is related
to the preceding one, but it is slightly different. On this
James says something that we would rather expect to be
true: 'The prayer of a righteous man has great power in its
effects' (Jas. 5.16). But it is the converse of this that is our
concern: clearly the prayer of an unrighteous man has very
little effect. The quality of the prayer isn't acceptable.

I would assume this to be true for two reasons. The first is
because the person who is 'unrighteous' must already be
out of touch with God, in a sense keeping out of God's way.
Obviously it's rather uncomfortable praying if you know
that there is an unsettled account with God that will have to
be dealt with at some time. To put it another way, if you
haven't paid the rent for the last five months, the last person
you are likely to go to for a loan is the rent collector. The
unrighteous person descends from praying to merely saying
prayers, from humbly consulting with God about the current problems to putting down a shopping list in the hope
that God will foot the bill with no questions asked. Then

secondly, since the God we are discussing is a God both of mercy and justice, he is rather likely to want to settle this unrighteousness business before attending to the prayer.

4. The fourth reason why prayer doesn't get answered is because *we can hardly be expected to ask God for the hard things of life*. Paul could scarcely have been expected to pray that God would stir things up in Jerusalem, conjure up a nice cosy riot and get him arrested and imprisoned; while he just might have thought that his arrest and appeal to Caesar was one way of taking a penniless preacher to Rome, he could scarcely have been expected to ask for the subsequent shipwreck. Inevitably we will want safe arrivals, comfortable journeys. But Jesus's words 'if it is possible' nearly always have to be added to our requests for safety and comfort.

While I was writing this book I had to take time out to visit a church in Sussex for the ordination of a former student. The journey by car took about two and a half hours, and it poured with rain the whole time. As I drove, with great care I hasten to add, I was thinking about this problem trip; why couldn't God have given me better weather? I wouldn't have objected to a light shower, but this was horrendous. And one possibility occurred to me: the weather was so bad that a good many people would stay in, cancelling their plans for journeys hither and yonder. And maybe among them was someone who most certainly, most desperately, ought *not* to go on his planned trip. Perhaps a trivial thought, but one day I may be allowed to know if that thought had substance to it.

At all events, what I am suggesting is that some of our prayers are not answered because we ask for what is entirely natural, and we simply couldn't ask for the hard way.

TWO MISUNDERSTOOD BIBLE SAYINGS

There are two statements made in the Bible that are often used to 'prove' the theory that we can get God to do whatever we ask. The first is the promise made by Jesus in John

14.13–14: 'Whatever you ask in my name, I will do it, that the Father may be glorified in the Son; if you ask anything in my name, I will do it.' This appears clear enough, and to require only that we add some such phrase as 'and this we ask in Jesus's name' (or, nowadays very often, . . . 'in the all-powerful name of Jesus') and then God has to do what we ask.

Here I have to ask Christians to behave as honestly as they do in every other area of life. Admit it: it doesn't work. We have all prayed many times 'in the name of Jesus' but have not got what we asked for. So there must be something wrong in our understanding of the proof text. Notice that there is no condition attached to Jesus's promise except that we should ask in his name.

Asking 'in the name of' or 'in my name' or 'in the name' are phrases that occur several times in the Gospels: for example in the context of 'receiving a child' in Matthew 18.5, and in the context of giving a drink of water in Mark 9.41. This appears to be something much more profound than the repetition of a formula: 'I receive this child in the name of Jesus', or 'I give you this drink of water in the name of Jesus'. What is meant is a situation in which the presence of Jesus is felt, known, so that what is being done is being done as he would do it. He would receive a child in a particular way, he would give a drink in a particular way. It is the 'Jesus way' of doing things that is intended.

Intercessory prayer, our ask-it, must be offered as Jesus would offer it. The prayer of Jesus would appear to have two characteristics: it was offered in an awareness of the will of God, and it would be offered in submission to the will of God: 'if it is possible, nevertheless . . ..'

This is enormously important, and it may well explain why it is that so many of our ask-its do not produce the expected answer. John Wimber has confessed that he has prayed for healing for thousands of people who have not been healed. And ultimately he has come to an acceptance of this cardinal principle of all intercessory prayer: 'A secret to healing prayer is that it comes from God having already touched our spirits; it is agreement with God about his will.'[3] Praying in the name of Jesus means praying as Jesus would pray, with power, of course, but that power is actually ensured by a knowledge of what God wants to do *in this case*.

Our problem is that we often want to produce a taxonomy of intercessory prayer, a classification of those principles which lie behind success, so that in any situation we may be sure of the rules governing successful prayer, usually in terms of the quantity of faith, obedience to Scripture, purity of living and so on. Such a taxonomy is a delusion. The one principle is alignment with the will of God.

That may at first appear to be an escape formula, but it is not. Although it is not possible in every situation to know God's will and to ask for it (Paul could scarcely have anticipated a shipwreck, still less have asked for it), still in most situations we can know. And the first step in intercessory prayer is prayer that asks to know God's will: 'What do *you* want in this situation?' That is where Jesus would start. That is what is meant by praying 'in the name of Jesus'.

The second statement often used to support the notion that prayer can be made to work automatically is found in Matthew 18.19–20: 'Again I say to you, if two of you agree on earth about anything they ask, it will be done for them by my Father in heaven. For where two or three are gathered in my name, there am I, in the midst of them.' There are several points of interest here. One is that Jesus has actually rephrased a current saying of the Rabbis, 'Where two or three are gathered to study the Torah, there is God among them.' Then there is the appearance of the formula referred to above: 'in my name', and also the surprising suggestion that if any two Christians should 'agree together' about anything at all, then God will do what they have asked.

Once again the principle seems clear, but once again honesty compels us to admit that it doesn't work. I first encountered this problem as a missionary. Our mission was anxious to begin a new work on the border between Ethiopia and the Sudan. The Ethiopian Government was not anxious to give that permission, probably because the border area was notably unstable. I was with a large group of missionaries, studying the Amharic language. On the basis of Matthew 18.19 we agreed together (many more than two or three of us) to pray for the necessary permit by the end of the week. But we didn't get the permit for several months, and I realised even then that we must have misunderstood what Jesus had said.

There is another feature of the Bible verse: the repetition of the word 'two'. If occurs twice in Matthew 18.16. In fact the whole of this part of the Gospel, from the beginning of chapter 18, is dealing with the question of greatness: who is going to be great in heaven. Jesus uses a child as an example of humility, and adds an illustration of God's pleasure in children (18.1–14). Then he turns to an example of pride: two adults with a disagreement that they are unwilling to resolve (18.15–20). Such disagreements are notoriously difficult to settle, but the promise in verse 19 is that even if the local assembly is unable to find a way of ending the disagreement (presumably by one or the other or both apologising, or by one or the other or both compromising), still if they actually *want* the problem to be resolved they can ask God to do it for them (of course granted that they both, or maybe both of them with their mediator, the two or three, want it), then it will be resolved. But Matthew 18.19 is not an invitation for any two Christians simply to gang up on God.

7
The God of the Two Testaments

C.S. Lewis, on the imprecatory element in the Psalms:

> . . . We must not either try to explain them away or to yield for one moment to the idea that, because it comes in the Bible, all this vindictive hatred must somehow be good and pious. We must face both facts squarely. The hatred is there – festering, gloating, undisguised, and also we should be wicked if we in any way condoned or approved it, or (worse still) used it to justify similar passions in ourselves.
>
> *Reflections on the Psalms*

In order to maintain what is being argued in this book, that God is righteous and compassionate, but that he is not omnipotent and does not will evil, we need a radically new way of understanding and interpreting the Bible. This is the main concern of this chapter, which will also suggest what that new way might be.

A CONFLICT OF CHARACTER: GOD IN OLD TESTAMENT HISTORY

The Christian Bible (the Jews also, quite properly, refer to their Scriptures as 'The Bible' but of course it has only what Christians call the 'Old Testament' in it) is the only authoritative source we have for understanding either our history or our theology. It has two parts, two 'Testaments' or 'Covenants', Old and New. Anyone who has seriously read through both Testaments will find it unsurprising that through the ages people have been perplexed by the apparent difference between the God revealed in the one and in

59

the other: the God revealed in the Law, with its bloody animal sacrifices (and how many Christians have stopped actually to envisage the scene of sacrificial butchery daily acted out at the Jerusalem Temple?) and in the prophets, demanding bloodthirsty revenge on whole towns and peoples, and in the warrior kings, and the God of compassion revealed by Jesus.

Let us pass over for the moment the very real problem of the righteousness of a God who demands the slaughter of tens of thousands of animals, not to satisfy hunger, nor even to take away sins, but simply as an object lesson for the peoples of a second dispensation, a new covenant. What we cannot simply pass over is the problem of an Old Testament God who not merely permits but positively orders the wholesale massacre of entire peoples, without mercy: men, women, children.

Take the example of a prophet, Samuel. He goes to Saul and informs him:

> Thus says the Lord of Hosts, 'I will punish what Amalek did to Israel in opposing them on the way, when they came up out of Egypt. Now go and smite Amalek, and utterly destroy all that they have; do not spare them, but kill both man and woman, infant and suckling, ox and sheep, camel and ass.' (1 Sam. 15.2–3)

In fact even the people rebelled against the senseless and wasteful destruction, and rescued some of the livestock. Saul spared the life of the leader of the Amalekite people, Agag. Samuel, when he arrived on the scene, realised what had happened:

> Then Samuel said, 'Bring here to me Agag the king of the Amalekites.' And Agag came to him cheerfully. Agag said, 'Surely the bitterness of death is past.' And Samuel said, 'As your sword has made women childless, so shall your mother be childless among women.' And Samuel hewed Agag in pieces before the Lord in Gilgal. (1 Sam. 15.32–3)

John Wenham, in his book *The Goodness of God*,[1] comments rather weakly '. . . it seems at first sight a very unpleasant incident'. It isn't an unpleasant incident, it is ghastly: Agag isn't merely executed, but 'hewed to pieces'. We cannot take refuge behind a cold and analytical and theoretical reference to 'the uncompromising nature of the Lord's demands' (John Wenham). At least part of the moral problem here is that Samuel, in the name of God, demands the punishment of the present generation for the enmity of a past generation, and of entirely innocent women and children at that. As the story is told it is quite clearly assumed that Yahweh would be well satisfied with all this slaughter.

The same principles seem to lie behind the execution of Achan in Joshua 7. Joshua had to take Jericho to secure his advance into Palestine. According to Joshua 6.2 it was Yahweh who gave him his orders. As transmitted by Joshua they involved the imposition of the *herem*, the ban, on everything and everyone in the city: 'the people went up into the city. . . . Then they utterly destroyed all in the city, both men and women, young and old, oxen, sheep, and asses, with the edge of the sword (Josh. 6.20–1). It was the Old Testament version of the eleventh- and twelfth-century crusades. Pope Urban II is Joshua and for Jericho read Jerusalem. During the assault on Jericho Achan looted clothes, gold and silver, dug a hole in the earth under his tent and hid them there. Inevitably his crime was detected:

> And Joshua and all Israel with him took Achan the son of Zerah, and the silver and the mantle and the bar of gold, and his sons and daughters, and his oxen and asses and sheep, and his tent and all that he had . . . and all Israel stoned him with stones; they burned them with fire, and stoned them with stones. (Josh. 7.24, 25)

Wenham tries to deal with the obvious contrst between all this and the teaching of Jesus (who was quite clearly opposed to using violence, even for good ends) by reference to Jesus's teaching on judgment and hell. But of course that is not the parallel. Achan had still to face *that* judgment and issues of heaven and hell. The real issue is whether God commands, wills, in *this* life what appears to be arbitrary and undeserved and cruel punishment. Final judgment will be his, and at it we may look for both justice and mercy. But war is a human activity of a fallen humanity. And although it is easy to agree with John Wenham that the church *as church* 'can certainly never rightly take up arms for the propagation of the gospel',[2] of course that is precisely what the Old Testament people of God purported to be doing. For them, killing, war, massacre, for the sake of the purity of the people of God was apparently justifiable.

THE BARBARISMS OF THE PSALMS

The psalms are usually taken to be the great repository of Christian meditation. And yet again and again as we read them we find ourselves horrified by the sentiments expressed. To me the most horrific is Psalm 137, which begins with words of great pathos and concludes with barbaric violence:

> By the waters of Babylon,
> there we sat down and wept,
> when we remembered Zion.
> On the willows there
> we hung up our lyres.
> For there our captors
> required of us songs,
> and our tormentors mirth, saying,
> 'Sing us one of the songs of Zion!'
> (. . .)
> Remember, O Lord, against the Edomites
> the day of Jerusalem,
> how they said, 'Rase it, rase it!
> Down to its foundations!'
> O daughter of Babylon, you devastator!

> Happy shall he be who requites you
> with what you have done to us!
> Happy shall he be who takes your little ones
> and dashes them against the rock!

It has been estimated that of the total of 150 psalms, eighty-four contain sentiments which Christians cannot possibly subscribe to, sentiments of malice, hatred, bloodthirsty threats and curses:

> It is not an enemy who taunts me –
> then I could bear it;
> it is not an adversary who deals insolently with me –
> then I could hide from him.
> But it is you, my equal,
> my companion, my familiar friend.
> We used to hold sweet converse together;
> within God's house we walked in fellowship.
> Let death come upon them;
> let them go down to Sheol alive;
> let them go away in terror into their graves.
> (. . .)
> But thou, O God, wilt cast them down
> into the lowest pit;
> men of blood and treachery
> shall not live out half their days. (Psalm 55)

Or Psalm 58.10:

> The righteous will rejoice when he sees the vengeance;
> he will bathe his feet in the blood of the wicked,

or Psalm 59:

> Thou, Lord God of hosts, art God of Israel.
> Awake to punish all the nations;
> spare none of those who treacherously plot evil.
> (. . .)

> consume them in wrath,
> consume them till they are no more,
> that men may know that God rules over Jacob
> to the ends of the earth. (Ps. 59.5, 13)

Or Psalm 69.24–8:

> Pour out thy indignation upon them,
> and let thy burning anger overtake them.
> May their camp be a desolation,
> let no one dwell in their tents.
> (. . .)
> Add to them punishment upon punishment;
> may they have no acquittal from thee.
> Let them be blotted out of the book of the living;
> let them not be enrolled among the righteous.

The Christian cannot endorse these words, and yet they are part of holy Scripture. Of course the true horror of these sentiments is that we have a sneaking approval of them: we want our enemies to get their come-uppance, we look forward to their eventual destruction. It is all part of what John Stott referred to as an evangelical *Schadenfreude* gloating, exulting over tragedy.

But it is wrong.

EIGHT PRINCIPLES FOR UNDERSTANDING THE BIBLE

A lifetime of teaching the Bible has been sufficient to convince me that it is not an easy book to understand, that the ideal of producing the perfect translation that will readily be understood by any reader cannot be realised. We are separated from its own times by 2,000 years, and in some parts by 3,000 years and more. To understand Isaiah we need to understand the history of the region: the conflict with Egypt and Assyria and Babylon; to understand Joel we must know something about locusts and about prophetic imagery; to understand Daniel we need to know about the rise of

Alexander the Great; to understand the New Testament we need to know of the status of Palestine, the history of the Herods, the authority of Pilate, the beliefs of the Pharisees. To have any hope of properly interpreting the parables of Jesus we at least must understand the Hebrew notion of the 'comparison', the *mashal* (and scholars have argued endlessly about that!).

So I admit that many of us are inevitably ignorant of such things and I am committed to our need of teachers. Unfortunately not all teachers are honest teachers. As 2 Peter 3.16 expressed it (nearly 2,000 years ago), referring to Paul's letters and neatly bringing together both the ignorant and the 'unstable', 'There are some things in them hard to understand, which the ignorant and unstable twist to their own destruction, as they do the other scriptures.' So I offer to those like myself who admit to being more or less ignorant, eight suggestions for correctly interpreting the Bible, Old and New Testaments. I had rather hoped to be able to construct ten and so to produce a new decalogue, but in fact found only eight. However if I do not have a new Torah it is perhaps more important that I have a new set of beatitudes. Happy are those who interpret their Bibles in conformity with them!

1. Remember that the Bible is divided into two parts, the Old Testament and the New. These two parts stem from the one God, but relate to two distinct periods: the period before the incarnation and the period after it. The Old Testament has a prophetic element to it, with prophecies looking forward to events which are still to come and which are only very vaguely perceived even by the prophets themselves: 'The prophets . . . searched and inquired about this salvation; they inquired what person or time was indicated by the Spirit of Christ within them when predicting the sufferings of Christ. . . . It was revealed to them that they were serving not themselves but you. . . .' (1 Pet. 1.10–12).

2. Remember the difference between the people of God in the Old Testament and the people of God in the New

Testament. The Old Testament people of God formed a nation, a political body. They were surrounded by other nations. There were wars and they couldn't stand aloof from them. They were invaded, attacked, and used as pawns in great empires. They had kings and generals and judges and politicians, as well as prophets and priests. They had an army. The people of God in the New Testament are scattered throughout the world, in virtually every nation:

> We may not count her armies,
> we may not see her King;
> her fortress is a faithful heart,
> her pride is suffering.[3]

3. The New Testament brings into sharp focus what was scarcely perceived at all in the Old Testament: the certainty of a last judgment. This makes an enormous difference to the problem of the righteousness of God. In the Old Testament the perception was that everything must work out justly in the here and now. It did not appear to (and that is the problem posed by Ecclesiastes, and partly answered by Job), but it must. God's people must be punished now, nationally, for the nation's sins, and the enemies of God's people, the Egyptians and the Syrians and the Philistines and the Babylonians and Amalek and the rest must be punished now if God's character as just and holy is to be preserved.

Under the new covenant we can see more clearly that that is not so: death is not the enemy we thought it to be, death does not close and balance the account. For all the injustice in the world it is at least possible that justice could come beyond this world. But of course the very notion of heaven and hell raises its own problem with regard to the character of God: does it conform with the character of God as revealed by Jesus that he should consign human beings to an eternal hell of suffering? That question will be dealt with in the next chapter.

4. The Bible is the inspired word, the authoritative scripture. It faithfully records human reactions, human emotions. And it is utterly honest. This is the record of what people thought and felt and did under the old covenant, and of their different thoughts and acts and feelings under the new covenant. Under both covenants people got it right some of the time and wrong some of the time. It is all faithfully written down.

To some people its very honesty is a problem. Muslims, in particular, find the honest record of David's lust for Bathsheba more than shocking; for the Muslim David could not have been like that. And that is one of the reasons why the Muslim world rejects both the Old and the New Testaments. Prophets don't sin. Well, in the Bible record the truth is told: they did sin, and from their sins we are expected to learn the appropriate lessons. We need to remember that no evangelist, no missionary, no preacher is above the possibility of sin. And we need to remember that when they (or we) do sin the Bible on the one hand points to the wrath of God against it, and on the other hand points to the way of repentance:

> Have mercy on me, O God,
> according to thy steadfast love;
> according to thy abundant mercy
> blot out my transgressions.
> Wash me thoroughly from my iniquity,
> and cleanse me from my sin!
> For I know my transgressions,
> and my sin is ever before me.
> Against thee, thee only, have I sinned,
> and done that which is evil in thy sight
> (. . .)
> Create in me a clean heart, O God
> and put a new and right spirit within me.
> Cast me not away from thy presence,
> and take not thy holy Spirit from me.
> Restore to me the joy of thy salvation . . .
>
> (Ps.51.1–4, 10–12)

That was David's prayer after his passionate affair with Bathsheba.

But how do we understand these violent passages from the Old Testament? Or even Paul's outburst in Acts 23.3? Paul was undergoing an informal trial, and Ananias, the Jewish high priest, ordered a bystander to hit him in the mouth: 'God shall strike you, you whitewashed wall!' responded Paul. It was strong stuff, and greatly provoked, but very different from Jesus in a very similar situation who said nothing at all.

As we read the psalms we remember that for the Jews of those days there was only the faintest glimmer of a belief in life after death: such as it was, it was shadowy, grey, fearful, not at all the perception that appears in the New Testament. And there was little in the way of an eschatological judgment: if sin was to be punished it must be punished now, and not in some determinate future.

Again, since God is a God of unswerving justice, then the ultimate punishment for flagrant sin must be meted out now, and the ultimate punishment was death: death in any case, because all have sinned, but a violent and horrific death, as fit punishment for horrific sin. And again since this was all self-evident it is appropriate for the righteous man to call on God to do what he has to do.

This philosophy that the more horrific the death, the more horrific must have been the sin that preceded and caused it, appears in the New Testament also. In Luke 13 Jesus is told about two incidents involving the violent death of some Jews. The first incident involved some Galilean Jews, who had offended Pilate in some way. Pilate waited until they came to Jerusalem, almost certainly at Passover, and when these Galileans were slaughtering their animal sacrifices he ordered the guard to attack and kill them, their blood mingling with the blood of the animals. To the pious Jew such a death must have appeared peculiarly repulsive: human blood and animal blood mixed together. Their conclusion was simple: such a horrific death must indicate horrific sin. And knowing this Jesus asks them: 'Do you think that these Galileans were worse sinners than all the other Galileans, because they suffered thus?' And to his rhetorical question there is an unspoken response: 'Yes, of course we think that they were worse sinners than all other Galileans.' But Jesus replies, 'I tell you, No' (Luke 13.2, 3).

The second incident related to the building of an aqueduct to bring water into Jerusalem. It was an important and valuable project, but like so many such projects it lacked the necessary funds. Pilate was involved in this case, too, taking Temple funds to pay for the aqueduct. Jewish opinion was almost unanimous in condemning him for it, and most Jews refused to work on the impious project. The project caused the collapse of the Siloam reservoir tower and the death of eighteen workmen.

Again Jesus asks his rhetorical question: 'Do you think that they were worse offenders than all the others who dwelt in Jerusalem?' And again the unspoken response: 'Of course that's what we think, otherwise why did they die like that?' Once more Jesus responds: 'I tell you, No' (Luke 13.4, 5).

Of course what we find frustrating is that Jesus did not go on to tell them what the real reason was for the horrific deaths of these men. He only tells them what it *wasn't*. As so often in his teaching Jesus leaves his listeners with an error corrected, but still with the responsibility of searching for the right answer to a difficult question.[4]

In fact the Bible is much more than a collection of proof texts which will enable us to find one-line answers to our multitude of questions. Just as Jesus, the Living Word, in leaving his listeners to think through their problems, paid them the compliment, due to people created 'in the image of God' with a moral conscience, of allowing them to find the answers, so the Bible, the written Word, allows us to come to it with our questions, and supplies us with principles from which to find the answers.

In other words the fact that 'it is in the Bible' and 'the Bible is the Word of God' does not mean that everything in the Bible is an expression of the character of God. Much of

69

it is an expression of the character of all humanity, Old
Testament humanity still waiting for that fuller revelation
which we have. We may understand how it was that they
got it wrong, but we need have no qualms as Christians in
saying that they did get it wrong.

5. In interpreting the Bible we must at all costs avoid the
error of quoting proof texts, single verses wrenched from
the context to prove a point. Even Luther was apparently
upset by the comment made by James: 'a man is justified by
works' (Jas. 2.24) and that 'faith apart from works is barren'
(Jas. 2.20). When the passage is pulled out of the co-text
(the rest of the text surrounding the words we are trying to
understand), James appears to contradict the rest of the
Bible's doctrine of the central importance of faith. Put it
back into the co-text and we can see that he does nothing of
the sort.

6. In interpreting the Bible we must take account not only
of co-text but also of context, the context within which this
particular verse was produced: for whom, under what circumstances, with what intention. To take my own favourite
example, a church in Blackpool, England, had a text boldly
displayed above its pulpit: 'I have a message from God for
thee' (Judg. 3.20). Hurled across the centuries in total dis-
regard of the original context it appears to be a message
directed by the preacher to the congregation. In fact it was
originally a sentence spoken by an assassin to his victim
moments before he knifed him!

7. In interpreting any part of Scripture we must pay attention to what is termed its literary genre, the *kind* of literature
it is supposed to be. Is it meant to be poetry, or prophecy, or
history? In particular is it apocalyptic, such as Revelation,
which is marked by a very confusing time line (see the
perplexing three and a half days of Revelation 11.9, 11 or
the 1,260 days of 12.6), and by quite extraordinary imagery
(see chapter 12, with its red dragon and pregnant woman).

And incidentally there is good reason to see in what is agreed to be the apocalyptic imagery of Revelation 12 firm ground for concluding that Genesis 3, to which it is deliberately linked, is not at all intended as orthodox 'history' but also as 'apocalyptic'.

8. Perhaps most importantly of all we need to relate any part of the Bible to the pivotal point of all history, the incarnation. As John's prologue puts it: 'the law was given through Moses; grace and truth came through Jesus Christ' (John 1.17). Before the incarnation all ultimate knowledge was shadowy, uncertain, in comparison with the blinding clarity that came with Jesus. In him was no mere prophet unsure of the significance of what he was saying, but God incarnate, shedding a blinding light on the human condition. Before the incarnation the people of God looked forward, but uncertainly, unclear as to what or who was to come. Since the incarnation we have all been looking back to a unique period of history, to God seeking to express himself in terms understandable to mere creatures of time, who are nonetheless creatures beloved by God.

8
Death

Screwtape on the death of a Christian killed in an air-raid in London:

> The more one thinks about it, the worse it becomes. He got through so easily! No gradual misgivings, no doctor's sentence, no nursing home, no operating theatre, no false hopes of life; sheer instantaneous liberation. One moment it seemed to be all our world; the scream of bombs, the fall of houses, the stink and taste of high explosive on the lips and in the lungs, the feet burning with weariness, the heart cold with horrors, the brain reeling, the legs aching; next moment all this was gone, gone like a bad dream, never again to be of any account. . . . Did you mark how naturally – as if he'd been born for it – the earth-born vermin entered the new life?
>
> C.S. Lewis, *The Screwtape Letters*

Death is usually seen by us as the end. The final curtain comes down. If the curtain comes down at the right time, when the play has reached a satisfactory conclusion, then we can walk away from the theatre moderately satisfied. But far too often the curtain comes down too soon. The potential of Act One has not been realised, the scenario we, the audience, had already sketched out in our minds will not take place, and nor will any other scenario for this particular actor.

Death is a consequence of some kind of cosmic fall, and as a consequence it remains for many of us a formidable enemy: inevitable, but to be resisted.

If that is true for us, with the historical event of the resurrection of Christ known to us, how much more was it true for the men and women of the Old Testament. For them although the dead were still there, somewhere, the somewhere was shadowy, fearful, cold, and oppressive. But death ought not now to be seen by Christians in this gloomy fashion: on the contrary it is the gateway to glory. It is, admittedly, an end of this life, with its uncertainties, disappointments, and failures, but it is the beginning of new life which contains none of those things. Paul dared to say outright that he would rather be dead than alive (2 Cor. 5.8)!

THE NATURE OF DEATH

We must all die. Death, if we must have a definition, is the final separation of the human spirit from its physical body. Actually, that definition says more than is at first apparent, for death is not the separation of the spirit from the body, merely its separation from the physical body. Christian belief is in the person as spirit-body, not spirit-with-a-body or spirit-trapped-in-a-body, but a unity of spirit and body. For the present it is an uneasy union between the spirit and a physical body, but ultimately it is to be a harmonious union between the spirit and a spiritual body.

Death is the final separation of the human spirit from its physical body. We have to say, therefore, that whatever insights we might be able to gain from so-called near-death experiences, they cannot be insights into death: the individuals concerned have not died. However, our knowledge of death comes from two sources, from the death and resurrection experiences of Jesus, and from the teaching contained in the Bible. Both affirm the reality of life beyond death.

This affirmation is important, and it requires a response from us, one of approval and acceptance, or one of denial. In turn each of these responses has consequences: we will order our lives in accordance with our beliefs. Of course I am not suggesting that those who do not believe in any kind of after-life must inevitably live the present life as immoral and dissolute hedonists. But they certainly will not live their lives in any awe or fear of God. Many people will respond that they do not have sufficient evidence about the life beyond to be able to make a decision one way or the other, in favour of life beyond death or in favour of death as the end. So why not postpone the decision?

The philosopher Blaise Pascal saw this personal decision as to the existence of something, some One, beyond life as crucial and also as inescapable. He pictured life as a journey, and life on board the ship is determined by the destination anticipated by the passangers. To the passenger who wants to ignore the question about the ship's destination Pascal simply responds: 'vous êtes déjà embarqué' – 'you're already on board'.

THE DEATH AND RESURRECTION OF JESUS

The example of the death and resurrection of Jesus is enormously valuable, but of course that event was unique. What we can see, however, is that the resurrection body that Jesus had carried all the powers of the old physical body plus new liberating powers. The new body could be seen, it could even be touched, it could eat. But it could appear and disappear and even pass through closed doors. It no longer suffered from the limitations of the physical body, but on the other hand it was not totally independent of that physical body: the resurrected Jesus was recognisably Jesus, he was more than a wraith.

Death is a gateway through which we all pass. As Paul expressed it in 2 Corinthians 5, it is stepping out of the temporary, fragile, human (father-and-mother-made) tent-like home and into an eternal home, owing nothing to human architects, builders or weavers. The new home is not a house, but a new spiritual body. The process takes us out of time, where life doesn't make sense and where God has largely been dethroned, into eternity, away from earth where we must still pray in expectation 'Thy kingdom come, thy will be done' and into heaven and the realisation of what we had longed for.

Arguably the most comfortable part of this portrayal of death is the provision of another house for the spirit. In

Christian teaching we are not absorbed into ultimate reality, nor liberated in a flameless *nirvana*, but we move out of a physical body and into a spiritual body which is vitally connected to, but fundamentally different from, the physical body. To quote Paul again, but this time from 1 Corinthians 15, the relationship between physical body and spiritual body is analogous to the relationship between seed and plant. As the tiny and even ugly black sphere that is the eucalyptus seed grows into the magnificent, spreading, shining, silver and green wonder of a great tree, so the human body is transformed into its eternal counterpart. Just as every tree is intimately related to the unique seed from which it grew, so every spiritual body is intimately related to the unique human body which gave birth to it.

To the Christian who knows, this is all that death represents: a doorway from time to eternity, a transformation from a weak, maybe even ugly, probably tired human and physical body into a glorious never-weary spiritual body. Contrary to much that most of us have come to believe, death is not the worst thing that can happen to us.

Of course it is the case that it is only a comparative minority who live out their lives in tranquillity and die peacefully. Death at its worst is violent and painful. It is often death that poses in its most poignant form the question: 'Why doesn't God intervene?' And yet it must be said that Gautama the Buddha had this much right in his analysis of the human predicament, life is characterised by suffering. So why should we fear death? Jesus himself confronted death with words that formed part of a prayer that was repeated by Jewish people, and still is, at the end of the day, a prayer of total quiet confidence, a prayer of tranquillity: 'Father, into thy hands I commit my spirit' (Luke 23.46). Even in death on a cross it was possible to rest in God, to be assured of the future.

While it is certainly true that in the Old Testament the grave was frightening and life beyond the grave was elusive, clouded, doubtful, in the New Testament we are out into the light: the horror of death is taken away, Jesus defeats its horror, Jesus leads his people fearlessly, triumphantly through its door and into the light that lies beyond.

As C.S. Lewis put it in *The Last Battle*, one of his Narnia Chronicles: 'Term is over: the holidays have begun.'

9
And After Death Comes Judgment

Screwtape on eternity:

> The truth is that the Enemy, having oddly destined these mere animals to life in His own eternal world, has guarded them pretty effectively from the danger of feeling at home anywhere else. That is why we must often wish long life to our patients; seventy years is not a day too much for the difficult task of unravelling their souls from Heaven and building up a firm attachment to the earth.
>
> C.S. Lewis, *The Screwtape Letters*

It appears to me quite clear that if this world is created by God who is righteous, fair, and just, then his justice is not experienced by us between the two apparent boundaries of birth and death. Humanism accepts that and settles for an unfair and ultimately meaningless world. Hinduism and Buddhism open up both boundaries and explain *dukkha*, the general unsatisfactoriness of life, as due to the *karma* brought forward from previous incarnations. Christianity and Islam open up the one door of death and set ultimate justice in the context of a universal post-death judgment.

Both religions recognise that beyond this world, beyond this universe of which the inhabited world is only an infinitesimally small part, we must exit from time into eternity and prepare for judgment to be passed on our individual lives. Judgment is 'eternal' judgment; at stake is the eternal destiny of each individual.

There are important differences, however, between the Muslim concept of judgment and the Christian concept. According to Islam we are to be judged by our fidelity to the

Quran and its central thesis, the one-ness of God, and by the extent to which our conduct has been in accord with Muhammad's own *sunna*, or practice. There is a further difference: Islam proposes a complex system of hells and of heavens, through which a soul might progress even after judgment, so that a soul sent to suffer in a kind of purgatorial hell could nonetheless eventually reach heaven. Indeed there is a widespread belief that almost all must experience at least the upper reaches of hell, but that all Muslims will ultimately attain heaven.

The Christian view is different. Fundamentally we are to face a judgment not of our behaviour, but of our faith, and in particular of our faith in Christ. To put it very simply, one is either 'in' Christ, or 'out of' Christ, and therefore either 'delivered' from the judgment or 'condemned' by it; one is either promoted to heaven or condemned to hell.

HELL AND A JUST GOD

Here once again we encounter a moral problem: hell. Once again to oversimplify the issue, how is it possible for the 'saved' in heaven to be happy knowing of the eternal torments of the 'lost', some of them relatives or friends, in hell? Or how can we reconcile the apparent sadism of a God who can consider inflicting eternal torment on his own creation with his character revealed in Jesus Christ, full of grace and truth, of endless mercy and boundless compassion?

For evangelicals one of the most important and valuable and controversial books to be published in the second half of the twentieth century was *Essentials*,[1] written as a dialogue between David Edwards and John Stott. It was important because David Edwards selected a number of issues crucial to evangelical belief, exposed the weaknesses of traditional presentations of those issues and then challenged John Stott to answer him. The agenda was not set by the evangelical partner in the dialogue, but by the self-confessed liberal, and it was not a verbal dual, which might subsequently be disowned by either side on some suitable pretext, but a considered, written dialogue.

Among the most valuable of the discussions were those on eternity and hell. The most emotive issue was that of the impenitent: does the concept of hell imply for them eternal conscious torment?[2] The alternative is what is termed annihilation. On the one hand the individual consciously suffers eternally, while on the other the individual is extinguished; on the one hand there is a belief in the immortality of the soul, on the other is a belief in conditional immortality, that humans may attain to immortality but are not created immortal.

It seems to me helpful to use John Stott's structure in considering the nature of hell. He has four arguments in favour of annihilation, and four objections to the first of them. The first argument is that the language of hell fire argues in favour not of pain but of destruction. While it is true that if I accidentally put my finger in a flame it will be extremely painful, if I leave it in the flame it will be destroyed. Thus the imagery of hell is the imagery of destruction, not of endless pain.

The Muslim would find some sympathy with this viewpoint. In fact Muhammad's opponents raised the obvious, if naive, objection to his idea of a burning hell and eternal torment, that the torment could not continue since the human body would be destroyed. Muhammad countered with the response that as soon as any particular body was destroyed by the flame Allah would create a new body, so that the pain could continue. (*Sura* 4.58–9)

To this first argument Stott notes four objections, relating to four passages from the New Testament: Mark 9.48, which speaks of a place where 'their worm does not die and the fire is not quenched'; Matthew 25.46, in the parable of the sheep and the goats, where reference is made equally to eternal life and eternal punishment; Luke 16.19–28, where the rich man cries out that he is in agony in the fire of hell; and Revelation 20.10, which states that in the 'lake of fire' the victims 'will be tormented day and night, for ever and ever'. To the four objections there are four responses. Firstly, although the fire continues to burn and the worm to destroy that does not necessarily mean endless torment, simply the endless work of destruction until it is complete. Secondly, although eternal life does mean unending enjoyment of God, and eternal punishment does mean unending separation from God, this latter does not necessarily mean eternal suffering. Thirdly, the story involving Lazarus and the rich man ('Dives') appears to be a parable with some specialised language in it ('Abraham's bosom') and it is also apparent that in the scheme of history we are dealing not with events after the final judgment but with events in the intermediate state, after death but before judgment. And fourthly it is pointed out that not only were those who were not written in the Book of Life consigned to the lake of fire, but so also was death, and even more surprisingly hades (Rev. 20.14), and since these two last were surely thrown there for destruction, certainly not for torment, the same should be true for all else thrown into the lake.

The second argument is that the vocabulary employed in the Bible in relation to the fate of the lost is the vocabulary of destruction. Jesus himself warned his listeners to fear God, who can 'destroy both soul and body in hell'. In the same sense believers who are being saved are contrasted with unbelievers who are perishing, and the verb used normally would mean 'being destroyed'. The narrow road leads to life, but the broad road leads to destruction (Matt. 7.13).

Stott's third argument invokes the sense of justice: is there not a serious imbalance between sin committed in time, and its punishment continuing through eternity? If the Torah laid down with so much precision the equality of sin and punishment ('an eye for an eye and a tooth for a tooth') we would expect to find the same careful balance in divine retribution.

And fourthly, Stott points to the clear expression of the love of God for the peoples of the world, and of the promise that ultimately 'every knee will bow to Christ' and God will reconcile all things to himself (John 12.32). It is difficult to see how this ultimate goal could be realised granted the existence of beings under continuous torment in hell.

However, while these observations lead Stott 'tentatively'[3] to favour annihilation and its concomitant conditional immortality, it does not lead him to universalism, the belief that ultimately there will be no one lost.

I have myself found the idea of conditional immortality increasingly attractive and Stott's arguments increasingly persuasive. And yet I still find myself committed to the traditional view, of an eternal hell paralleling an eternal heaven, and of human beings once created having eternal destinies. The annihilation of a unique individual created in the image of God appears to me to be a defeat of the divine which is even greater than the continuing existence of hell.

We would all agree that the imagery of a lake of fire is imagery only: what the image signifies I do not know. But we would probably also agree that heaven and hell both take us out of time and into eternity, and therefore into a life which has that timeless dimension for which we have no vocabulary at all. We speak of the horror of souls in endless torment, day after day and year after year, but in eternity there are no days, no nights, no years, no time. Our moral problem, once it reaches eternity, takes us into a new dimension which defies human language with its surrender to time and its tenses and moods.

One further point needs to be made here: it is clear to me, although not to all Christians, that if hell is populated it is populated with those who have overtly rejected Christ. There are throughout history many such. There are those who are too sophisticated to put faith in the Galilean peasant; those so enmeshed in the search for pleasure that Jesus can only be seen as its antithesis; those who have their own gods – the acquisition of wealth or honour or power – and inevitably find it impossible to put Jesus alongside them; those of corrupt mind and will, who prey upon others, some of them on the microscopic scale, our petty thieves, pimps, and murderers, and some on the macroscopic scale who foment war and bring millions to ruin. All could find mercy, but few ask for it.

But what of those who have never had the chance of following Christ?

THOSE WHO HAVE NEVER HEARD THE GOOD NEWS

On the question of those who have never had the opportunity of following Christ I have written elsewhere[4] using ten theses to set out what I believe. Rephrased but unchanged in their import my theses are as follows.

1. It is unjust to condemn humanity for disobedience to a law they have never heard and for failure to avail themselves of a remedy they did not know existed.
2. The death and resurrection of Christ is sufficient to deal with all sin, for all time. No other remedy is needed or possible.
3. Those who have not heard of Christ are not completely without the possibility of knowing God. He has shown his nature in creation, where his deity can be perceived (Rom. 1.20). And Acts 17.27 indicates that God has created the world precisely so that people should long for its Creator and find him!
4. Just as those who encounter Christ may either receive him or refuse him, so those who encounter God in creation may either accept him or reject him, and just as those who reject Christ are rightly condemned, so those who reject God's self-revelation are rightly condemned.
5. Just as those who receive Christ are saved from the consequence of their sin by his death and resurrection, so those who submit to God's revelation in creation are saved from the consequences of their sin by Christ's death and resurrection.
6. People may be saved while they are in one of the world's religions, or when they profess no religion at all, but no one can be saved by religion.
7. Salvation comes to us exclusively through Christ, but an overt knowledge of Christ is not required for salvation. It is

helpful to add here that almost all Christians are agreed that this thesis is true for particular classes:

- Children who die before being able to understand Christ's love.
- People suffering from mental disorders which similarly prevent them from understanding the Christian good news.
- The peoples of the Old Testament, Abraham and Isaac and Jacob (Matt. 8.11), are in the kingdom, and yet did not hear the good news.

8. The understanding and reception of God's self-revelation in creation is not an unaided human act, but is as God-given as is our response to the preaching of Christ. As John puts it the light shines on everyone, and it is the light of the Logos, the light of Christ, that enables God's self-revelation to be perceived.

9. While this opens the way for people outside the reach of any Christian witness to find salvation, it does not deliver the Christian from the responsibility to 'go into all the world' to speak of Christ. It is true enough that without hearing the gospel of Christ preached people might gain heaven, but they would still be denied the possibility of living a truly human life.

10. Summarising, I suggest that any attempt to deal with the very real problem of the vast majority of those who have ever lived but who never heard the good news must conform to what we know in Christ of the character of God: his justice and his mercy, his compassion and his righteousness. The view long held by many evangelicals that those who have not overtly heard the good news cannot be saved seems to run contrary to that divine character.

For me, and for many who have heard his story, the story of Esa raises the issue in its most poignant form. I learned of Esa while researching in southern Ethiopia for my first book. He lived around the turn of the century. He never encountered a preacher, yet Esa suddenly announced to his people that they must abandon their traditional religion, put an end to sacrifices and the worship of the moon, and instead worship God the Creator. He knew no more than that. In the event thousands of his people followed him. Somewhere in the 1920s he died, still without hearing the good news, but the people continued to observe his teaching. Then in the 1930s there came an Ethiopian preacher, and the people recognised that what he was saying filled out the little that Esa had been able to tell them. They became Christians.

And here is the question: were they saved, because they heard, and was Esa lost, because he didn't? According to traditional evangelical belief that is so. But according to the ten theses this is a classical illustration of the saving effect of God's deity revealed in creation.

AN OBJECTION: HUMAN LOGIC

There are Christians who believe that it is not merely misleading but actually wrong to use human logic, human intelligence, and human categories, when discussing the character of God. In the words of the Preacher, 'God is in heaven, and you upon earth; therefore let your words be few' (Ecclus. 5.2).

In fact this is generally speaking the view that is taken of logic in Islam. Since Allah is greater, he must also be greater than language, and any human word used to characterise Allah must at once take on a fresh meaning because it refers to Allah. Ultimately this simply closes down all talk about God since all words are rendered meaningless by their context.

The Muslim hermeneutic is effectively used in dealing with the dogmatic assertion of the Sovereignty of Allah. For Islam he is omnipotent, directly (and not merely indirectly) willing the events of human history. He *wills* cancer and earthquake and famine and accident and rape and murder. And if we question the concept of the compassion of God, and especially the righteousness of God, the response is simply to assert that when those words are used of Allah they become different words. In the early centuries of Islamic development it was simply asserted: 'What Allah does is right.' It was the later philosopher Mutazilites who recognised the moral problem and insisted by contrast that 'Allah does what is right', with the recognition that making such a statement conveyed exactly the same meaning as would the same statement made of any other.

At this point, at least, the Christian theologian agrees with the Mutazilites: God does what is right. And the Christian theologian also agrees that we know the difference between right and wrong. Human logic is by no means infallible, but it is not valueless or positively misleading. Most particularly we would say that the act of redemption itself refines the human intellect, and opens up new areas of clarity of thought.

Of course if the human mind is fatally flawed, then all processes of thinking are ultimately meaningless; all human decisions based on the thought processes are also flawed, and we cannot even read the Bible with confidence.

AND HEAVEN

I have elsewhere listed what I see as six characteristics of heaven,[5] so here they are:

1. God is at the heart of it. Not pleasure, not eternal feasting, not sex. God is the focus of heaven.
2. Heaven marks the end of that pain and suffering, those tears and sorrows that in some sense have been the theme of this book.
3. And related to that, but still distinct from it, heaven is totally free of evil. Everything there is clean, purified. Christians who read these words will understand what that means: no longer will we be embarrassed, upset, pained by the sheer dirtiness, the grubbiness with which we are surrounded day after day. That smirk that I remember so well, on the face of a famous TV comedienne as she earned a

cheap laugh, not with a smutty joke but with a bit of crudity: there will be none of that.

4. Heaven is a place of light, of radiance: there is no night there, only a pure shining radiance, the glory of God.

5. Heaven is Eden restored. In that Old Testament story there is a garden and a fruitful tree of life and a river, and in heaven it is all there again, but free from the imminent expectation of the coming of temptation.

6. But if heaven has God as its focus it is also true that heaven is a place of celebration: it is marvellous, beautiful, a place of rejoicing, but emphatically it is a Jesus celebration, a celestial wedding that even C.S. Lewis, who abominated parties, could enjoy.

It is all so marvellously summed up in Revelation 21:1–4:

> Then I saw a new heaven and a new earth; for the first heaven and the first earth had passed away, and the sea was no more. And I saw the holy city, new Jerusalem, coming down out of heaven from God, prepared as a bride adorned for her husband; and I heard a loud voice from the throne saying, 'Behold, the dwelling of God is with men. He will dwell with them, and they shall be his people, and God himself will be with them; he will wipe away every tear from their eyes, and death shall be no more, neither shall there be mourning nor crying nor pain any more, for the former things have passed away.'

10
Is God Helpless?

Screwtape on the circumstances surrounding a Christian's repentance:

> The asphyxiating cloud which prevented your attacking the patient on his walk back from the old mill, is a well known phenomenon. It is the Enemy's most barbarous weapon, and generaly appears when He is directly present to the patient under certain modes not yet fully classified. Some humans are permanently surrounded by it and are therefore inaccessible to us.
>
> C.S. Lewis, *The Screwtape Letters*

I have suggested that if we insist on believing in a God who is compassionate, loving, just and omnipotent, then we are forced to reinterpret our ideas of compassion, love and justice. The world is and always has been filled with suffering, wars have always happened, disease has always been there, famines, earthquakes, floods, storms have always brought disaster to humanity. If God is omnipotent then he is responsible for it all. I have further insisted that it won't do to play with some imagined distinction between what is willed by God and what is in the permitted will of God. If he is omnipotent and permits evil then he is responsible for evil. He is not good.

I have also said that in the Old Testament we are confronted necessarily with an inadequate theology, precisely because clarity awaited the coming of the incarnation. Only in Jesus are the mysteries of life and death, and of life beyond the gateway of death, demystified. The imprecatory psalms, the demands that God step into Israel's affairs in bloody vengeance, the notion that God would command the destruction, the massacre, of men, women and children for crimes that were not their own, must all be attributed to the limited revelation available to the prophets and priests and kings of the old covenant. They cannot represent the God revealed to us in Christ.

I have argued that God cannot intervene in our lives so that we only do what we ought to do, because that would deny to us that very element of choice that makes us human, and would deliver us into a world that was utterly unpredictable.

But that does not mean that God does not intervene and cannot intervene. It is true that God does not intervene on the macro scale: he does not intervene regularly, always, everywhere, but that does not mean that he does not intervene. I believe in miracle, in God stepping in to do something that is, to us, inexplicable.

Miracle is, in fact, distributed rather sparsely through the Bible. There are the miracles connected with the Exodus, there are those connected with Elijah and Elisha, and then there are the miracles connected with Jesus and then with the early church. And yet the sum total of them is small. The Bible does not present us with a picture of a fairyland world of magic wands and three wishes. It is still, largely, a world of regularities. But interspersed through those regularities are the exceptions: God intervening.

INTERVENTION: THE MICRO SCALE

Do miracles happen? Have they ever happened? What do we mean by a miracle? This last is by no means an easy question to answer: what might have appeared to anyone living 1,000 years ago to be miraculous, television, for example, to us is no miracle at all. Science has advanced and made television possible, and no doubt science will continue to advance and make more things now not even imagined matters of everyday experience. But at least one constituent of miracle is that it is for the time being inexplicable.

The following two 'miracles' are detailed in Geoffrey Ashe's *Miracles*. A seventeenth-century series of miracles of levitation are associated with a Franciscan monk, Joseph of Cupertino. He flew repeatedly, and hundreds of witnesses attested to these flights. He even levitated during an audience with Pope Urban VIII. One of those who witnessed his flying was the mathematician Leibniz. And yet there appears to be no particular point to his flying. It appears to have happened, but no one was any the better for it, with the possible exception of a man who was mentally unstable, but was apparently cured when Joseph took him on a flight.

One of the best attested of miracles is the dancing sun of Fatima in Portugal, and this took place in the twentieth century with 70,000 witnesses. Three children, Lucia, Francisco and Jacinta, claimed to have seen the Virgin Mary, who promised that a miracle would occur in Fatima on 13 October 1917. An enormous crowd gathered: some to see the miracle, some to note that the promised miracle did not occur. Among these last were the journalists, and especially Almeida, the editor of a secular anti-clerical newspaper, *O Seculo*. They all saw the same thing: the sun danced, whirled, spiralled, and continued to do so for nearly ten minutes. As it appeared to spiral closer and closer to the earth so the people began to panic: and then the sun returned to its place. The phenomenon was visible twenty miles away, although nothing unusual was recorded by the Lisbon observatory. Almeida, still a sceptic, nonetheless confirmed the inexplicable event. But again we can see no particular point in this miracle.

There is no shortage of accounts of healing miracles, stretching back into the New Testament and forward into 1982 (and, doubtless, beyond). Bede's *The Ecclesiastical History of the English People* records innumerable examples of healing which he suggests were signs of the presence of God and a compassionate response to human need, resulting in the conversion of England. Fractured bones were healed, the blind regained their sight, even the dead were restored to life. Donald Bridge, in his valuable *Signs and*

Wonders Today, chronicles not only those miracles, but precisely parallel miracles in the twentieth century. Rex Gardner, a Fellow of the Royal College of Obstetricians and Gynaecologists, in his book *Healing Miracles*, records the 1982 healing of a Pakistani woman named Kamro, who at childbirth was hypertensive and anaemic, and was haemorrhaging steadily because her blood would not clot. This condition normally requires massive blood transfusions, and these were not possible in Pakistan, the blood was not available, Gardner comments: 'we may estimate that Kamro lost at least her complete blood volume, possibly two or three times over. But despite this her condition did not deteriorate. She behaved as though God was replacing the blood as quickly as she was losing it.' The details of the case were confirmed in writing by Dr Ruth Coggan, herself a FRCOG, missionary of the Church Missionary Society and daughter of the former Archbishop of Canterbury.

But in all of these examples of healings one is still left with the realisation that they are no more than a token for faith, an indication that God is there, that God does still have compassion for us. And yet in the main the problem of human suffering remains unresolved.

God does not intervene on the macro scale because it would turn a world of bearable regularities into a world of unpredictability, it would turn us from women and men charged with the moral responsibility for our own decisions into automatons capable only of what is 'right' but at the same time denied the very category 'right', since right and wrong indicate moral choices. But yet God does intervene on the micro scale, although even by the testimony of the Bible, infrequently. He has healed the sick, given sight to the blind, restored broken bones, even raised the dead.

INTERVENTION: THE MACRO SCALE

But what about the macro scale? To the Christian there are three points of intervention: at creation, at the incarnation, and at the *parousia*, the revelation of Christ at the world's end.

This universe is no cosmic accident. Whatever laws have moulded its development through the millennia, it is God who began it all. This assertion (and, of course, it cannot possibly be proved) is of real importance since it then presumes a purpose behind the act of creation. That purpose is somehow and in some measure thwarted by the fall. But the *parousia* and the summing up of all things in judgment, in reward, in heaven, in hell, is the ultimate assurance that God is, after all, on the throne. The world is not entirely and madly out of control: it is hurtling towards a creation goal.

Between those two acts of macro interference stands the incarnation: the entry of God into the world. Again I insist, if the Jesus story is merely the story of another prophet, another teacher, another miracle worker, then I surrender the Christian position. It is of no interest to me: I have teachers and to spare. But that is not the Christian message; and let us remember that there is no new revelation, no new evidence that will enable us to fabricate another, alternative Jesus of history. Of course the bookshelves are regularly stocked with rapidly selling latest titles offering just such a Jesus: but they come and they go, because there can be no new evidence, merely the shifting around of the evidence we have, the arbitrary removal of this bit or that in accordance with 'what people today can believe'.

The fact is, of course, that whatever scholars in their academic towers may say of us, modern men and women, like their predecessors, can believe in all sorts of things: in television and radio, in computers and fax machines, in good and evil, in levitation and reincarnation and transubstantiation, in bent spoons and hazel twigs, in Almighty God and the devil, in slaying in the spirit and homeopathy, in talking to the flowers and walking on the moon. There is nothing in the Bible account of the incarnation that modern men and women *cannot* believe, although a good many people throughout history have stated firmly that they do not or will not.

What Christianity claims is in some sense the response to the question raised by this book, 'is God helpless?' God in

Christ became one of us, lived among us, deliberately chose (that is the point of the incarnation) to be one of the poor so that no one could ever again say that God did not understand. He came here, and lived here; he healed people and so demonstrated the compassion of God. He healed very few, but he healed some. He gave back life to very few, but he gave back life to some. He showed that God was not helpless. And at the end he did two things: he accepted the ultimate meaninglessness, unfairness, of life and accepted an undeserved death on a cross; he died, and then walked through death into resurrection life. He showed us what it would be like to live the authentic human life, and then he showed us the comparative unimportance (for us who follow him) of death.

THE NEW COMMUNITY OF FAITH

Even that is not all. In returning alive to his followers Jesus established a new community, a community of compassion. The church is to be in some sense his new body: seeing as he would see, feeling as he would feel, weeping as he would weep, healing as he would heal. No, even Jesus was not able to heal all the sick he encountered. In Nazareth he was able to accomplish very little: he healed a few people, but could do nothing of great significance, because of the unbelief of the people (Mark 6). My guess is that this explains the comparative rarity of healing in the cynical Western world, and its comparative frequency in the Majority World. In Ethiopia, at one time, my nearest neighbour was a man who had never walked until the day he became a Christian. He was born a cripple, grew up without taking a step and then in his twenties encountered an Ethiopian evangelist, received Christ, stood up and walked. The church expected such acts of power, the people expected them; of course God was not helpless.

God sent his new community, the church, into all the world, to preach good news: good news concerning the kingdom that would one day arrive in power; good news about the kingdom that is already here in microcosm, touching a life here and another there and assuring us that God is not helpless. Good news, also, of a compassionate community that shared in the sufferings of the world, bore those sufferings too, and bore them patiently, knowing that death is not, after all, the worst thing that can happen to us, but rather that it could even be the better thing for us. Good news that over against time there is eternity, and there, and there only, we shall see the justice of a God who for too long has been dethroned, whose compassion has for too long been refused.

As I have said elsewhere:

> To be a missionary is to confront human *dukkha*. It is to hear the cry of the world. Even the cry which sheer hunger and exhaustion and despair stifle at its birth. It is to hear that cry as God hears it, and to respond, not with more books and more international conferences, but with a truly biblical praxis . . . a praxis which incarnates the will of God in an as yet unredeemed world.

> Mission is more than the multiplying of missionaries or even of churches. It is rather the confrontation of the human condition, of human meaninglessness, and in the name of God so resolving it that God's Kingdom comes. The Kingdom is the *entelechy* [the fulfilment] of the Church. The mission of the Church is to be that *entelechous* flower out of which the perfect will come.[1]

Notes

INTRODUCTION
1. See Kenneth Surin, *Theology and the Problem of Evil* (Blackwell, 1986). This offers a very readable yet profound study of the prolem of evil.

CHAPTER TWO: WHAT RELIGIONS SAY
1. Vatican Council II, *Nostra Aetate*.
2. From Radhakrishnan (trans.), *Bhagavad-Gita* (Blackie & Son, 1970, India), chs 1 and 2.

CHAPTER THREE: ABOUT GOD
1. John Wenham, *The Goodness of God* (IVP, 1974), p. 44.
2. Michael Green (ed.), *The Truth of God Incarnate* (Hodder & Stoughton, 1977), p. 128.
3. Colin Gunton, *The One, the Three and the Many* (Cambridge University Press, 1993), p. 181.

CHAPTER FOUR: GOD'S WORLD
1. John Betjeman, 'Christmas', in *Church Poems* (John Murray, 1981).

CHAPTER SIX: BRINGING THE TWO TOGETHER
1. H.E. Fosdick, *The Meaning of Prayer*.
2. C.S. Lewis, *The Screwtape Letters* (Fount, 1993), ch. 9.
3. John Wimber, *Power Healing* (Hodder & Stoughton, 1986), p. 214.

CHAPTER SEVEN: THE GOD OF THE TWO TESTAMENTS
1. *The Goodness of God*, p. 133.
2. *The Goodness of God*, p. 144.
3. C.S. Rice, in *Hymns Ancient and Modern Revised* (William Clowes, 1950).

4. For a scholarly consideration of the problems of identifying the historical setting of these two incidents in Luke 13, see I. Howard Marshall, *The Gospel of Luke* (Paternoster, 1978), pp. 552–5.

CHAPTER NINE: AND AFTER DEATH COMES JUDGMENT

1. David Edwards and John Stott, *Essentials* (Hodder & Stoughton, 1988).
2. *Essentials*, p. 314.
3. *Essentials*, p. 320.
4. Peter Cotterell, *Mission and Meaninglessness* (SPCK, 1990).
5. Peter Cotterell, *Dealing with Death* (Scripture Union, 1994).

CHAPTER TEN: IS GOD HELPLESS?

1. Peter Cotterell, *Mission and Meaninglessness*, (SPCK, 1990) p. 278.

Bibliography

Marilyn M. Adams and Robert M. Adams, *The Problem of Evil* (OUP, 1990).

Geoffrey Ashe, *Miracles* (Routledge and Kegan Paul, 1978).

Donald Bridge, *Signs and Wonders Today* (IVP, 1985).

Donald Carson, *Divine Sovereignty and Human Responsibility* (Marshall Pickering and Baker Books, 1994).

Peter Cotterell, *Mission and Meaninglessness* (SPCK, 1990).

——, *Dealing with Death* (Scripture Union, 1994).

Stephen Davis (ed.), *Encountering Evil* (T and T Clark, 1981).

David Edwards and John Stott, *Essentials* (Hodder and Stoughton, 1988).

Rex Gardner, *Healing Miracles* (Darton, Longman and Todd, 1986).

John Goldingay (ed.), *Signs, Wonders and Healing* (IVP, 1989).

Paul Helm, *The Province of God* (IVP, 1993).

Pope John Paul II, *Crossing the Threshold of Hope* (Cape, 1994).

Kenneth Surin, *Theology and the Problem of Evil* (Blackwell, 1986).

Keith Ward, *Divine Action* (Collins, 1990).

John Wenham, *The Goodness of God* (IVP, 1974).